£1-50

THE HOUSE OF BREAD

Ken Hornsby's first job was in a public library, which he put to good use by writing *Is that the Library speaking?* an amused look at the foibles of the library system and the people who use it. He then moved on to become an advertising copy and script writer, latterly as a creative director in a multi-national advertising agency and then starting his own consultancy. During this time he wrote *The Padded Sell*, a wry look at the advertising industry. He has also published a novel which was shortlisted for The Guardian junior fiction prize; a remembrance of his experiences in the war; and had two plays performed publicly.

BY THE SAME AUTHOR

Is that the Library speaking?
The Padded Sell
Wet Behind the Ears
A Child at War

PLAYS

Don't Mind Me
The Waiting Room

THE HOUSE
OF BREAD

THE HOUSE
OF BREAD

THE FULL STORY
OF THE BIRTH OF JESUS

KEN HORNSBY

Published by FreeHand Publishing Limited
175 Munster Road, London, SW6 6DA
Registered Office Centurion House, 37 Jewry Street, London, EC3N 2ER

First published 2006

ISBN-10: 0-9551847-0-3
ISBN-13: 978-0-9551847-0-3

Design and production John Nicholls
Typeset in Bembo
Printed and bound in England by William Clowes Limited

TO ANNE

Who never thought she'd be an editor as well as a wife and mother

PREFACE

There is surprisingly little information in the Bible about the events surrounding the birth of Jesus Christ: less than a couple of pages in total.

Only two of the Gospels mention it at all, and each was written for a different audience: Matthew for the rich (hence the Kings from the East - or "wise men") and Luke for the poor (the shepherds). Probably neither was written until some seventy or eighty years after the event. It is hardly surprising if the memories were hazy or the events embellished.

Historically there are many inaccuracies.

The shepherds would not have been in the fields in December; they and their sheep would have been tucked away from the weather in barns or caves.

There is no record of any census being held at that time, though there was one six years earlier and another six years later.

There were no inns in Bethlehem because Bethlehem was not on the trade routes.

The three kings from the east would not have been kings; kings did not do things like that. "Wise men" is certainly nearer, since such travellers were astrologers and priests, soothsayers and sorcerers. They had a poor reputation and were always looking for ways to improve it.

The Slaughter of the Innocents is not recorded in Bethlehem. It is more likely to be referring to a documented cull by Herod of his own family, who were optimistically celebrating his death two years before it occurred.

But does any of that matter? Undoubtedly *something* happened. It is well-nigh certain there was a holy man at about that time who had many followers and said radical things. Mary and Joseph were asked to believe the (almost) unbelievable; if they were at first uncertain, no-one should be surprised. However close to the facts the Gospels are, what happened at that time is believed by many to be one of the world's greatest events. As such it deserves to be spelled out in much greater detail.

In this book I have sought to put the story into proper historical and geographical context, to sort out some of the factual inaccuracies, to log the proper chronology, even to hint at explanations for the apparently inexplicable. The bones of the story are exactly as in the New Testament; the background is from a variety of sources. It is just the personalities themselves who have been coloured in and rounded out, based on character and lifestyle as recorded by historians.

If it happened, this is how it might have happened.   KH

CONTENTS

CHAPTER 1

MARY

Zerubbabel's Temple in Jerusalem was not a beautiful building. Purely rectangular, it looked bleak and forbidding. An outside altar on which sacrifices were made stood before it, and immediately behind the altar a short flight of steps led up to two large rounded pillars framing the entrance to the building itself. Around the outside stood a number of bronze stands where the money-changers operated. Above was a small open terrace at the front and a much larger one across the whole roof behind with a walkway around it.

Three people stood before it. The two older ones felt a little uncomfortable, a little threatened by its size and appearance. The child just looked astonished.

They were there to give thanks for the first time as a complete family. Only a few years earlier Anna and Joachim had given up all hope of children. They were both well over forty and concluded they were never going to be blessed. But after all the years, their prayers were suddenly answered and at the age of forty-one Anna had conceived at last.

They, their friends and family, were convinced that this was God's will and were certain that the baby was destined to spend its life in the service of the Lord. But since serving the Lord was man's work it was a shock when the baby turned out to be a girl. It left the new parents at a loss; but even so they named her after Moses's sister, the most holy woman they could think of.

The tiny three-year-old was standing stock-still, her little hands clenched tightly into fists, staring at the temple.

"Mary?" her mother asked, amused at the sight.

Mary - or Miriam, to give her real name, of which Mary was an affectionate short form - seemed transfixed at the sight before her. A half-smile on her lips, her mouth a little open, she was both astonished and thrilled. Saucer-eyed, she looked up at her parents then back to the building in front of her, unimaginably larger than anything she had ever seen.

Nothing of the plainness of the five hundred year old temple seemed to trouble her. "Temple," she stated, as though she knew exactly what it meant and with the satisfaction of one who has arrived at a place always longed for. "Temple," she said again happily.

Leaving her mother behind she stepped forwards a few feet and stopped again, ignoring the people around her crowding into the Temple Mount on their way to worship. Anna and Joachim exchanged glances with each other, taken by surprise at the reaction in their daughter. Then they too stepped forward, prising her little fists open to take each of her hands in theirs, and entered the outskirts of the temple.

They had brought her to the temple now they felt she was old enough, even though this was a place for men, not women. Something inside them told them to ignore the usual constraints. Without even discussing it they knew this was what they should do. And Mary's reaction that morning, from the very first moment she set eyes on the temple, told them they had been right.

Somehow she seemed to be leading them. She appeared to have an instinct where to go, marching round the courts inside, slipping through the crowds, ending up - as though she knew they were there all the time - before the ancient scriptures engraved on the walls within.

Staring at marks which meant nothing to her, her eyes widened with pleasure. Anna and Joachim were standing next to her, a little bemused, when a voice broke in. "So you've brought my little girl at last."

They turned to find Zacharias, the husband of Mary's much older cousin Elizabeth and a priest of the temple, standing behind them.

"Mary," said Anna, "look who's here!"

Mary turned and gave a huge grin of delight at seeing her godfather in this wonderful new place. The priest picked the girl up and hugged her. "And what do you think of all this, precious child? Your first time in the temple. Is it not wonderful? Do you not feel the power and comfort of our great God all around you? Is this not a truly blessed place?"

Joachim grinned. Words like this were too much for a three year old. He smiled as he took the child back from the priest. "What's he talking about Mary? That's a bit grown up for you, isn't it?"

But Mary looked solemn. "Temple," she said again, "Mary likes Temple. God's place." She wriggled to get down and Joachim lowered her and caught Zacharias's eye.

"Well - she seems to understand something of what you say."

"The child understands," said the priest. "This is her place. She will spend much time here."

"But she's a girl," said Anna.

Zacharias looked steadily at her. "There is a point at which this does not count. There is a point in communion with God where it doesn't matter whether it's boy or girl, man or woman. The holy temple is a unique meeting place between the Lord God and his servants. Men and women can enter that holy state, whatever people usually believe. It goes beyond anything we understand. Since she was born so late in life to you I have always believed that Mary would be one of those chosen to be close to God - and I think you have too. Let us bless her and have faith."

Joachim put an arm around his wife Anna. "We prayed for many years for the blessing of a child, as you know," he said to the priest. "And we always believed he or she would be special. We thank you for your words and the Lord God for the blessing of our little Mary."

As Zacharias had predicted, Mary found her second home in the temple. Learning to read early, she devoured the scriptures and spent hours talking to the priests and scribes. She showed an astonishing understanding for someone so young, and if people were surprised to find a girl rather than a boy behaving in this way, they came to accept the sight of the slight young lady who found it natural to spend so much time there.

But as the years passed, attitudes changed. No longer did people just smile at the sight of the deep conversation between child and priests but realised there was something deeper developing.

Everyone liked Mary. She was easy to talk to. And though she was devout in her beliefs, she was only pious in the best sense of the word. All those who knew her were impressed by her understanding of the scriptures, her approach to life, and - even at such a tender age - her wisdom.

When asked about her, Zacharias would say, "There has long

been a belief that true wisdom resides in woman, not in man. For longer than I know, through many generations, it is passed down that feminine wisdom is divinity made human. It is no surprise to me that Mary has inherited this God-given gift. You will see, she will become great among the people of Israel."

And indeed it seemed that Mary already had a destiny marked out. For as she neared her twelfth birthday, only months away from the age when her parents would be considering marriage for her, she already knew she was going to be different from other girls. And one day she summoned up enough courage to tell her parents.

"Dear mother - dear father - I have been talking with Zacharias and praying in the Temple and I have reached a decision about my life."

Anna and Joachim were by now accustomed to Mary's unusually adult language but even they were a little taken aback by this solemn pronouncement. They looked at her in silence as she went on. "I am going to devote my life to God. And among many things this means one in particular. I know you would be thinking about marriage for me before long, but this is not what I intend. I believe that to serve God in the absolute way I want to means I must always remain chaste. I will never marry. I will never know a man in that way."

Anna sat down in shock. It was the destiny of every Jewish girl to marry and bring children into the faith. More: it was their duty. She could not see how Mary could possibly reconcile her decision with the centuries-old requirement of their religion.

"But how can this be Mary?" said Joachim, speaking Anna's thoughts for her. "This is not the way for a Jewish girl. You know what you have to do. I respect your love for God, of course we all do. But leave such devotion to the priests. It is priests who choose to deny themselves marriage for greater purity. And even then they do not have to. Your duty is to extend our race, you must know that."

But Mary did nothing more than smile at them and shake her head.

The parents could think of nothing to say. They looked at each other, puzzled and dismayed.

In the end Joachim felt he had to say something. But all he could think of was, "Oh Mary, little Mary..."

CHAPTER 2

THE DREAM

Within just a few months of that conversation Joachim decided he was becoming too old for the hard life of a farm worker and retired to take his family sixty four miles north to the tiny town of Nazareth in a remote region called Galilee. Fewer than four hundred people lived there, and Anna and Joachim found it easy to settle down. They bought a minute farmhouse a little outside the town. It needed a lot of patching up, but Joachim had plenty of time on his hands. He needed a certain amount of technical help and chief among those he employed was a carpenter named Joseph.

Joseph was a widower of about thirty five. His wife Esther had died a few years earlier, leaving him with two children to bring up. Joses and Juda were now early teenagers and still living in his tiny house which doubled as a workshop.

Joseph's parents got on well with Anna and Joachim. And it was not surprising that after a few years they began to look at Mary as a potential new wife for their son. Mary had little say in this; it was the job of the man's parents to find him a bride. Mary of course knew Joseph well; liked him but couldn't say she loved him. In fact, she didn't want to love anyone, as her parents knew too well. She had been heartbroken to leave Jerusalem's temple but found herself a new home in the synagogue in the heart of Nazareth. She still wanted to keep herself chaste but as she grew older the pressures of family and religion combined to make her accept that this was just not realistic.

Eventually she agreed to the betrothal. She underwent an embarrassing and very personal check with the doctor to confirm that she was a grown woman in all respects. Her father Joachim had to make a statement to Joseph's parents to guarantee her capability in the household and that she would be willing and hardworking in her wifely duties. He also had to promise that she was a virgin; and as such received twice as high a dowry. To all intents and purposes a contract was then in existence. She was just sixteen.

Mary had not wanted to get betrothed or married. But once she knew she had little option, being a practical girl she decided to make the best of it. She did like Joseph; he treated her with respect and she soon came to respect him too. He was an excellent craftsman, industrious and reliable. He cared well for his children. He would be a good husband. There would be little money, but amongst their acquaintances who did have money?

One warm afternoon Mary left her parents' house and set off to the town. She had two aims: she was going to the synagogue, and then on to Joseph's house to share with him some astounding news she had just received. She still couldn't fully believe it and kept turning it over in her mind.

As she was wandering slowly towards the marketplace, still reflecting on the news, the sound of shouting woke her from her reverie. She looked across the marketplace and saw a small crowd gathered around the steps of the synagogue.

On the steps stood the Rabbi and just below him a woman of perhaps thirty or thirty-five. In her hand she held a goblet from which she had obviously just stopped drinking. On her face was a look of horror and fear; on the ground a quickly spreading stain from the goblet's liquid which she had clearly wasted no time in spitting out. As the girl watched, the woman's face crumpled and the shouts of the crowd grew more ferocious. Beside the Rabbi another man had raised his fist in the air and was looking around the crowd for support.

Mary stood stock still, in her mind a mixture of understanding and disgust. It was a scene she had seen a number of times before and it never failed to disturb her. Immediately changing her mind about where she was going first, she headed away from the centre of the town and towards the hill where she knew she could find peace and solitude.

But she immediately came across another problem: that rather attractive Roman soldier Panthora. He had caught her eye a number of times as she walked about Nazareth and although she had always managed to avoid him it was clear he was watching her. And now she could see him again, walking in her direction. Quickly she changed her route and hurried behind a couple of small cottages and onto another path that would take her up the hill. She hid for a moment and looked back down the slight rise she had just climbed. Panthora was nowhere to be seen. Breathing a sigh of relief she started her climb again.

As she went higher she could hear the crowd outside the

synagogue begin to chant, "Death to the adulteress, death, death..." followed by the ominous cracks as people began throwing their stones.

She hated the whole business. She knew what had happened. Whether with good reason or not, the woman's husband had suspected her of adultery and started the usual procedures. He had enlisted the Rabbi's assistance, who had publicly given the woman the goblet of disgusting liquid to drink. Had she been able to swallow it completely and retained her composure, she would be deemed to be innocent. But if, as had obviously happened on this occasion, she had been unable to swallow the liquid, or it had made her vomit, she would be declared guilty. The husband then had two choices.

If he were an exceptionally lenient and forgiving man, he would simply have written out his own letter of divorce, posted it publicly on the walls of the synagogue, and the marriage would be over. The woman would have no future, since she would be ousted from her family home and no other man would ever take her.

But the more usual procedure was death; death there and then by stoning. And that was what was happening now. And what Mary could not stomach.

Something within told her the test was unfair and the treatment barbaric. She didn't know why she felt this, since there was nothing unusual in the scene, nothing that differed from a procedure that had lasted for centuries. Yet Mary had always failed to see why the way that a stomach reacted should be any reasonable sort of indication whether a marriage was sound or not.

As she climbed she could see the town spreading out beneath her; and the farther away she got the better it looked. The shabby, forlorn-looking little houses with their white renderings took on a picturesque air. The squat dome of the synagogue lost its threatening look. And at the centre the main street widened, opening into the marketplace and making a circle around the community well. The little bazaars and workshops, including Joseph's, were squashed in tight and clearly visible, though the people walking about - especially the little crowd around the synagogue - seemed more insect-like than human. The streets were thronged with men, women, children, camels and donkeys. Even at the distance and height she was, Mary could hear the buzz of voices and footsteps, the sharp and mechanical sounds of builders and tradesmen at work, the terrifying cries of the crowd around the woman at the synagogue.

Putting her hands over her ears, Mary continued her climb into the mountain, seeing the heart-shape of the lake of Galilee now coming into view, with its patches of dark and light blue and pale green. The hills bordering the lake were decorated with palms, olives, fig trees and vines. And all around the lake edges were the signs of the various trades attracted there: the boat builders, the dyeing factories, the potteries, the fish-curing sheds.

And in the even farther distance she could just begin to make out the thin dusty lines of the caravan routes and other important highways that met and crossed by the lake and then continued their journeys towards Damascus and Egypt one way, Jerusalem and Antioch the other.

Finally Mary found the curve of bushes she had been making for; a natural retreat she had often take advantage of when she wanted to think quietly to herself. She found herself saying a prayer for the woman below, by now perhaps already dead; if not, lying blood-soaked on the ground still surrounded by the venomous crowd.

For a good hour she stayed there. To drag her thoughts away from the events of the synagogue, she pulled the piece of rolled papyrus with the astonishing news from the tucked pocket in her robe and stared at it in amazement yet again, as she had done countless times since she had received it from the traveller from Hebron. The excitement started to envelop her again and after a while she began to feel strong enough to go down again to find Joseph.

But she was caught again. Rounding a clump of bushes at the beginning of the little town she ran straight into Panthora. And this time there was no escape.

Although they had seen each other often enough, they had never spoken before. For a Roman, this was exceptionally good behaviour. But now he did speak. "Well little one. And where are you hurrying to so busily?" There was an annoying touch of patronage to the question but she dared not take exception. Roman soldiers were not noted for their forbearance.

Fortunately she had a good answer. "To my betrothed, Joseph of Nazareth, the carpenter."

"Betrothed eh? That's a shame. What a waste."

She should have been upset. But she couldn't quite decide what to make of him. The words he used did not quite match the person he seemed to be. Perhaps he felt he ought to play a role. He was obviously flirting but there was something open and honest about his face, and somehow he hadn't annoyed her.

"I must go," she said, unable to avoid returning his smile.

"And what do they call you?"

"Miriam," she answered, feeling it would be sensible to keep it formal. And also thinking that as no-one knew her as that in Nazareth it would be less likely to be a problem if he ever talked about her.

"A good name," he said, "a good biblical name. I shall remember you Miriam." He stood watching her as she hurried away, carefully choosing her route so as not to pass the synagogue.

In the town she pushed her way through the bustle to Joseph's little workshop. As usual the door stood open but though his tools were spread about over the workbench in the doorway and on the floor inside, Joseph himself was not to be seen.

She looked about with a little affection; at all the tools he loved, many inherited from his father, who had lived and worked here for upwards of forty years before handing on the business to his son. No less than his father, Joseph took a deep pride in his workmanship and his craft. On the bench the adze for shaping the woods, the bow drill and bits for the pegs and dowels which held so many of his pieces together. On the shelf behind, the latest tool, his pride and joy, the spoke shave for the most carefully calibrated shapes. In the background, the trusty old lathe, surrounded by wood shavings. And resting against the walls, various offcuts of sycamore, olive and oak. Standing about too were parts of ploughs and yokes in various stages of construction. There was also one long straight board, which looked suspiciously like the beginnings of a coffin. She thought of the woman at the synagogue again but knew it wasn't for her. She would be buried with no ceremony in unconsecrated ground.

Mary tried to put it all out of her mind and called: "Joses? Juda?" Receiving no reply from the boys and guessing where she might find their father, Mary crossed the tiny street and went into the blacksmith's shop almost opposite. As she had anticipated, Joseph and

Jesse the smith were working together as they so often did, their trades frequently interlocking.

Before them on the floor was a cistern lid; Joseph had obviously finished his part of the construction and was now helping Jesse fix the metal surround.

Both looked up as Mary entered; Joseph the older, Jesse six or seven years younger but towering over his slimly-built friend. As ever Mary marvelled at the difference between them: Joseph intense, thoughtful and withdrawn; Jesse open-faced, unguarded, ever-cheerful.

"Mary!" As usual it was Jesse who spoke first, a great roar of a greeting, followed by a huge arm momentarily clutching her warmly around her shoulders. From Joseph, nothing but a shy smile of welcome.

"You two..." said Mary, enjoying the familiar sight of the pair of them working quietly and happily together. But the contrast between this easy scene and the violence of the emotions at the synagogue steps killed the smile on her face.

"Mary?" Joseph saw the look and wondered.

"Oh - there's a stoning..."

She didn't have to finish the sentence. Joseph knew her feelings about such things and indeed rather shared them.

"Come along," he said, and then to Jesse, "you're all right now, aren't you?"

"You go," said Jesse, "I can manage now we've got the rim on."

Together Mary and Joseph crossed back over the street and into Joseph's house where he gently embraced her before realising she was bursting with news.

"Mary? What's happened? Something exciting? It looks like it."

She grinned, pulled the papyrus from her pocket and thrust it out to him.

"Read it. It's from cousin Elizabeth. A traveller brought it late last night."

Joseph perched himself on the sawhorse and screwed up his eyes to read. Mary stood before him, the smile still on her face, barely able to contain her excitement. Joseph finished reading, lowered his hand with the papyrus still in it, and grinned back, if a little puzzled.

"It's hard to believe, isn't it?" he said. "Wonderful though, absolutely wonderful."

10

Mary's face was lit up, the upset of the stoning forgotten for the moment. "It's so exciting. After all this time. Elizabeth will be so thrilled. I'm going to see her."

Joseph was surprised. "Whoa, wait a moment. Hebron's seventy or eighty miles away. That's five or six days travelling. Down beyond Jerusalem. How're you going to manage that? A girl on your own?"

Mary was not to be daunted. "I'll find a way. I'll find some group to travel with. But I must go, I must see her." She sat down, staring at the papyrus which Joseph had handed back to her. "Elizabeth. With child. After all this time."

Joseph was too delicate to add, "And at her age too". But it was true. Elizabeth's mother, sister to Mary's mother Anna, was far older than Anna; she had had her daughter very young and Elizabeth was now well past normal child-bearing age. Elizabeth and her husband Zacharias had long given up hope of any son or daughter.

It had all but blighted Elizabeth's life. With Zacharais a priest at the temple she could see no reason why God should have refused them a baby. It was reasonable to assume that Zacharias was blameless, so it only left her, paying penance for some misdeed or unbelief she was unable to think of.

"God has been so good..." said Mary, almost to herself.

"Eventually," said Joseph, quite to himself. But his face was soft, watching Mary smiling as she read the letter again. They were almost exactly half way through the normal betrothal period of a year, almost half way towards the point when they would start living together. He wondered how they would find it, living in the tiny house together. It was no more than three rooms. The front one, opening on to the street, was his workshop. The back one, just up a step and very slightly larger, was sitting room, bedroom, kitchen, all in one. And then there was the other tiny room beyond that, where the two boys slept. It had been a terrible squash before, what with his widowed father, Esther and the two young children. And now before long there would be a wife again. And, God willing, a child or children too. Well, Joses and Juda were already teenagers and perhaps it wouldn't be too long before they decided to move on somewhere.

Leaving Mary still dreaming, he went into the living room to find cheese, oatmeal biscuits and grape juice for their lunch.

Back home in the early afternon, Mary busied herself with the chores of the house.

Her parents were old now and able to do less and less for themselves. The small dowry they had received from Joseph's parents had come in useful, but Mary still had to eke out the little money they had by making clothes for people nearby, as well as all their own. She was expert at distaff and spindle, deftly making yarn and thread from the raw wool of the hillside sheep. Then she would weave the yarn into cloth to make the tunics and fringed mantles that were worn by man and woman alike.

She could also grind the grain, bake the bread, make cheese and curds. Her life was a busy one and she often wondered how she would manage once she and Joseph were married and she had her duties to carry out in his house too. But "God would provide" she believed and prayed that between them they could all cope.

It was Friday afternoon, the start of the Sabbath, and in every household in Nazareth people were busy, performing the various duties that had to be done before sunset. Mary cleaned and washed, prepared meals for the following day, refilled the lamps, made sure her parents wanted for nothing. So that by the time the evening stars began to appear and the hazzan from the synagogue called everyone to prayer with the three blasts from the ram's horn, she was already tired enough to sleep deeply.

But when she finally did wrap the coverlet around her after the cheerful family meal and the recitation of the Kiddush it was not to an easy sleep.

The excitement of Elizabeth's letter kept her awake at first. Difficult as she found it herself to believe the wonderful news, she was sure that Elizabeth was finding it harder still. As she drifted in and out of sleep, visions of her cousin with the new baby floated before her, accompanied by the usual alternate sounds of crying and contentment. She saw Elizabeth resting in one of the few seats in the little house, the child at her breast, smiling a smile of happiness and fulfilment. And as she dreamt she saw visions of herself in the same state, with an attentive Joseph hovering in the background.

The force of this vision must have pushed its way through her sleep, for Mary found herself awake again, staring into the darkness, wondering what fate held for her and Joseph in the future. She felt herself poised on the threshold of a new life and even in repose she felt her whole body alive with expectation.

Without realising it she slipped back into sleep again and found herself in conversation with someone, a striking-looking man of about her own age but somehow with a wisdom and worldliness that she knew was missing in herself.

His first words took her aback. He told her she was favoured by God, that God was with her, that she was blessed among women.

This was not the sort of dream she had ever had before, and even though she was asleep and her emotions subdued, she felt a tremor of alarm course through her body. What could this mean?

In an attempt to get the conversation back to some sort of normality she started to say how she envied her cousin making preparations for the wonderful event of giving birth when she realised the man was not listening. Instead he was telling her something of immense importance. Elizabeth's new baby was to be no ordinary baby. He was to be a prophet, preparing the way for the Messiah who would soon be coming.

The sensation of being on the edge of a new life that she had felt earlier suffused her again and somewhere between sleep and wakefulness she could feel herself glowing with excitement. Somehow, despite the astonishing news, she found she could believe what the man had said about Elizabeth's child being a prophet without difficulty. Perhaps this was sleep intervening. Perhaps the quiet power of the man made her just accept what she was being told.

And like any young woman whose friend or relation became pregnant it stirred the same feelings within herself and for a moment this overwhelmed that news. She said again to the man how she envied Elizabeth and how she could barely await the intervening months before she and Joseph were married and she too could look forward to carrying a child in her womb. And then came the even bigger shock.

"But you are already carrying a child in your womb," said the man.

Sleep and dreaming could be a world in which normal problems didn't exist. Mary at first felt only delight at the news, although somehow it didn't make sense.

"But we are not yet married." At this point it was nothing more than a fact she was pointing out. There was no thought about how it would seem to the outside world.

Then the man said words that, had she not been dreaming, would have seemed so strange that she would have ignored them as impossible. "You do not have to think about that. This will not be an ordinary baby. I have already said, you are favoured with God. This will be the Son of God. The child will be called Jesus and as it is written in the scriptures he will come of the line of David."

At first the very simplicity of what the man said, the completely matter-of-fact tone in which he said it, made it easy for Mary to accept. And it had some ring of truth about it: for Joseph was indeed of David's line, as were so many in Judea.

Then the shock set in.

Herself, the quiet and modest Mary, mother of the Son of God? Mary, who was not married yet and had been with no man?

She felt she had to reply. For an instant her natural good manners took over and somehow the words came out without her thinking: "I – the handmaid of the Lord? Then let it be as you say."

The words she spoke might have sounded easy. But they did not represent what she felt. Inside she was in turmoil – and in fear. Could it really be that she was chosen to bear such responsibility? She felt shocked and alarmed but at the same time that tremendous elation she had felt earlier. It was only when she next awakened from the disturbed night that the worries started.

Her first thought was simply to ascribe the message of the man to the absurdity of the world of dreams. But as she lay on the floor under the warm sheepskin coverlet she stared at the low ceiling and knew something had happened. If she was truthful, she had known something was happening for days. Any experienced mother would have recognised the symptoms and feelings. Mary the innocent was just confused.

The words the man had spoken in the dream were still firmly, exactly, in her mind. "This will not be an ordinary baby, this will be the Son of God." Mary found herself again overwhelmed. How could this be true? How could she be pregnant? And just as amazing, how could she – why should she – bear the Son of God?

And then an awful memory came back to her: the sight and sounds from the synagogue steps. For a terrible moment she saw herself in that position, with Joseph standing over her, the Rabbi administering the potion, the crowd calling for her death. Quite unable to reconcile that situation with also being the mother of the Son of God, Mary screwed her eyes tightly closed and pushed her hands over the side of her head, trying all she could to shut the impossible situation out of her mind.

And then nature came to her rescue and she fell asleep again, this time with no dreams to disturb her.

CHAPTER 3

THE MAGICIANS

An extraordinary sight was to be seen five hundred and fifty miles to the east: two men in their seventies and one rather younger struggling their way up a hillside in the early morning darkness.

"I'm getting too old for this," said one of the elderly man, his white hair and trailing beard swaying in the wind.

"Not you," said Kaeso, giving his companion a gentle shove from behind and laughing encouragingly.

But old man Melchior was right. Healthy as he was for his age, it was hard for him to trail up the mountain before first light every morning. Summer and winter he followed the same routine, his grumbly old servant Benyosef finding it ever more difficult to keep up too, with his hands full of charts blowing in the wind.

But Kaeso knew that once Melchior stopped his morning climb it would be the beginning of the end for him. His daily scrutiny of the heavens, the interweaving of the stars and the planets, the plotting and monitoring of their movements - all were the bread of life to the old magician. He had left many of his activities behind now; no longer did he practise his magic spells or his fortune telling. And it was years since he had last created an augury for the future. Now he just concentrated on his astrology, still anticipating - as he had done for over fifty years - the sign in the heavens that the ancient prophecy was about to be fulfilled.

Kaeso, nearly twenty years younger, had been accompanying Melchior up and down the mountain for nearly ten years. And recently he had been sharing Melchior's excitement as they saw the planets moving - so slowly - into the position in the constellation of Aries which would provide the sight they had been waiting for.

"Come on old man," said Kaeso cheerfully, trying his best to keep the atmosphere light. "And you too Benyosef; only another ten minutes." In truth Kaeso was worried about the speed they were moving at lately. If they weren't careful the new dawn would have broken before they had time to mark the new positions on their charts. And the old man's eyes were certainly not what they were. In fact if it weren't for Kaeso himself goodness knows how accurate the charts would be these days.

He was grateful that Melchior's childhood friend Caspar was expected before long. They all knew that the planets Jupiter, Saturn and Mars were moving into place and Caspar wanted to be there with his friend to chart the last movements. Once Melchior and Caspar got together Kaeso could relax a bit. It was all very well being chosen to be the old man's chief assistant but it was beginning to be a bit like a nursemaid's job these days.

Benyosef was having trouble with the charts. It was always like this in the winter; the winds were up before they were and the old servant's hands were slow with arthritis these days. More than once Kaeso had had to sprint back down the slopes to rescue some of the papyrus as it whirled away from them.

Kaeso looked upwards and to the east. He could see the beginnings of light spreading towards them. He decided it was too late for niceties and grabbed the charts from the servant's hands.

"Here we are then," he said, in a vague effort to cover up his impatience.

Melchior settled himself down on his usual rock and peered upwards. Kaeso gathered up the piece of flat wood they left on the mountain and arranged it carefully across the old man's knees, smoothing out the first chart and laying it flat. He thrust the charcoal into Melchior's hands and sat down beside him. It was a delicate matter these days; he had to allow Melchior to believe he was in charge while at the same time checking what the old man was up to and correcting him when he wasn't seeing clearly.

Together they stared into the heavens, Kaeso trying to look both upwards and sideways at the same time, checking that Melchior was recording positions properly. Melchior's eyesight seemed good this morning, Kaeso was relieved to see, and he relaxed a little.

The new marks that Melchior were making were exactly as expected. Indeed there should never be any surprise if they were doing their job properly. Every day every planet moved a little; but always in the same arc as the previous day. The trick was recognising which planets were moving forwards and which back. That of course meant they appeared to move at differing speeds. And just to make it more interesting still, they *were* moving at different speeds.

But they had it all planned out. They knew precisely where each planet should be in relation to each of the others and to their stars at the centre. The satisfaction came from the daily confirmation that they really did understand how the heavens worked.

But now there was something different to be excited about. Something that was so different, that had been waited for for so long, that it was hard to believe it was really happening. In the next few months a whole school of Magi would be gathering; perhaps a dozen of them, all astrologers, all priests, all bubbling with the quiet excitement of believing that a historical prophesy was about to be fulfilled.

"All right?" It was a needless question, since both Kaeso and Melchior knew it would be all right. Painstakingly, the old man marked the new positions, noting how the arcs were still intact as the planets moved along their predestined routes.

"You're sure this is it?" asked Kaeso.

"This is what?"

"You know."

They didn't need the conversation. As the three planets moved towards each other they knew in their bones that what was shortly to come was what the Eastern world had been waiting for: the words of the prophets about to be fulfilled. The importance of the constellation Aries the Ram - "The ruler" - was well known. A meeting of the planets under this sign would be interpreted as a signal of a great man's birth. And as the three planets moved closer the astrologers knew what else would happen. The light that would emanate from them would become the brightest in the sky.

The astrologers perched up the mountain were not Jews; but they recognised the importance of the event to the Israeli nation across to the west. If a king was to be born, the Magi would be the first to know and were determined to be the first to visit and pay their respects. For wasn't that the duty of those who foresaw the future and could predict the effects on man? (It was also the requirement of a body of people who didn't enjoy the best of reputations and were looking for every opportunity to improve them.)

Kaeso glanced across at the old man, who was totally absorbed in what was happening above. They had had endless conversations about the importance of the movements of these planets. How the Babylonian tradition referred to Jupiter as the planet associated with kings and Saturn the protector of the Jews. How there would be one specific day when Jupiter would rise in the east precisely when the sun sets in the west - the achronychal rising - and thus appear to shine at its very brightest. And now that very day was beginning to be in sight.

"When do you think?" It was another of those conversations they did not need. Kaiso knew just as well as Melchior.

"Four months?" Melchior had finally answered. It was not the working out of the calculation that had delayed him. It was not difficult to predict when the combined glow from the planets would be at its strongest, to provide that great white light in the sky that would seem to be the fulfilment of the prophecies concerning the Messiah. It was the enormity of acknowledging the fact at all.

Even for an old man who had spent his entire life discussing the movements of the planets and what they foretold, the fact that they were within just a few months from the day an entire historic nation had been waiting for for centuries was too momentous a thought to be spoken easily.

Kaiso nodded. He knew what was going on in the old man's mind, and hoped that Caspar would soon be here; it would be someone to take the pressure off him.

The morning light was rising fast. Night went and dawn came in a matter of minutes in that part of the world and Benyosef was already beginning to collect up the charts when they heard shouting from below.

Kaeso looked down the slope and screwed up his eyes, trying to make out who was approaching them slowly up the hill and calling out at the same time.

"Who is it?" asked Melchior, even less able to see than Kaeso.

"I think...yes, it's Jairus. Wonderful. Jairus!"

Kaeso started down the mountain, delighted to be reunited with one of his oldest friends. They threw their arms around each other, bestowing the traditional kisses and standing back to look at each other.

"Jairus! It's...how long? Must be months."

"Half a year my friend. But you're not surprised to see me, are you? Not with all this going on?" Kaeso's friend gesticulated towards the heavens before turning back to greet Melchior who had by now arrived beside them. "Melchior! What a day it will be!"

"It will, it will..." Melchior's face was crumpled. The anticipation was beginning to affect him strongly. At his age he more and more easily gave into emotion, and it only needed another colleague to exhibit his own excitement for him to find a lump in his throat for a moment.

Together the three of them, arms around each other, descended the sharp hill. Behind, unsure whether it behove him to be as excited as his masters, old Benyosef struggled his way downwards, fighting to keep the charts under control and cursing to himself when they got between his eyes and his feet so he could not protect himself from the potholes and boulders that, he swore, set out to hinder his progress. He would be exceedingly glad when this whole light in the sky business was over and they could return to some sort of normality.

Back down the mountain another surprise awaited them.

As they approached Melchior's house they saw two elegant and powerful Arabian horses standing outside, both steaming from their journey in the early morning sun.

Melchior craned forwards, compressed his eyes to focus with his hand and said, "Do I see what I think I see?"

"I think you do," said Kaeso, even more delighted. So Melchior was to have not one but two of his best friends with him. "I think it's Balthazar."

"Melchior!" Balthazar, black-skinned and heavily bearded, rushed from the house to embrace his lifelong friend.

"Balthazar! It's so good to see you. And no need to ask why."

"When do we go?" Balthazar was not wasting time.

Melchior laughed. "Not so soon my friend. It'll be a few months yet I think."

"Show me the charts. Is it really months? Can't we go now?"

Melchoir laughed again. He considered that his old friend had reached the age of fifteen and stayed there for the last fifty years. But the enthusiasm was infectious.

"Come inside and I'll show you. To leave now would be to get there before the event. Come. There is a lot to do before we set off.

Do you know how many of us there will be? At least ten I think, perhaps a dozen. But come inside, eat and drink and rest. Tonight you shall go up the mountain with us and see the stars come out and put your own marks on the charts."

CHAPTER 4

ELIZABETH

When she finally awoke, for a moment Mary couldn't remember the dream; she just knew that something odd had happened in the night. She started to say a prayer of gratitude as she did every morning for the goodness of God and for being spared another day - when suddenly memories of the dream drenched her thoughts.

But as so often with dreams or mid-night ideas, what seemed hard and fast at the time seemed much less so in the cold light of morning. Staring at the low ceiling above her head, the whole idea was preposterous. And yet, not very surprisingly, she could not forget it.

But there were more pressing things to do.

She was determined to visit Elizabeth, despite the difficulties of such a journey and the worry it would cause Joseph. She started by asking around the little town to see if she could find anyone heading in the direction of Elizabeth's home town of Hebron, some seventy miles away.

She was lucky. Hebron was just seven or eight miles past Jerusalem and as she had hoped it was not too difficult to find a little group travelling south towards the big town. She would have to find someone else to accompany her over the last few miles; and even if she couldn't and the worst came to the worst she felt she might risk it on her own. It was, after all, only a couple of hours' walk.

There were seven others: two walking, two on donkeys, one on a rather fine Arabian horse and the final two sharing a cart. Mary herself managed to borrow a donkey from a friend. She had barely sat on a donkey before and guessed that before the journey was over she would feel both aching and sore.

It would not be comfortable with the weather either. It was towards the end of December and the white roads, so burningly hot for most of the year, were now cold and uninviting. It had been an exceptionally dry summer, but now the rains were coming to compensate; necessary to carry the countryside through the farming year ahead but disastrous for those travelling on foot. It was hard enough to find lodging for the nights in any event, but with sodden clothing life was twice as difficult since there was very little chance of drying things. The compounds in the caravansaries or beside the small wayside inns would quickly become waterlogged and the dirt and mud would get everywhere.

Also Mary was not feeling particularly well.

Fortunately the majority of the journey - as far as Jerusalem - would be on quite good roads, for it was only a short way before the track joined one of the main trade routes along the solid paved road provided by the Romans. It was therefore also a route for the government postal system and was reasonably well provided with inns for the messengers taking the rulers' instructions from one end of the empire to the other. And lastly it offered passageway for the army, with all the heavy equipment they trailed around behind them.

It was also relatively safe; one of the enduring results of Herod's rule. Because for all that every Jew in the land hated the politically appointed king of Judaea they had to admit he had achieved an astonishing success with law and order. And though it could still be dangerous for unaccompanied travellers to walk or ride the small roads and tracks over the mountains, he had succeeded well in controlling the brigands and bandits on the big roads.

It was two further days before the little troop set out for Jerusalem. Joseph had raised all the obvious objections to Mary going off by herself, but she was an independent girl and had reassured him as best she could. He waved a sad goodbye, sure he wouldn't see his betrothed for several months. Mary hadn't decided how long she would be staying; it would be wonderful to be there for the birth but perhaps that would be too long. She would decide that later. Meanwhile she had seen to it that her parents would be well cared for by neighbours, found herself surprisingly sad at leaving Joseph, prayed fiercely for courage in the face of the difficulties of the journey, and bore silently the memory of the curious dream.

The road from Nazareth towards Jerusalem was largely uphill and progress was slow. Mary had recognised a young woman in the party called Zara, also travelling on a donkey, and the two of them talked or stayed silent happily together as they made their slow way past the Judean hills. Covered with fig, olive and vine trees, the hills stood to each side of them, providing a colourful backdrop against the bleakness of the weather.

On many of the hills stood small villages, rows of mud box houses neatly surrounding the hilltops, youngsters working or at play, grown-ups going about their business as farmers or spinners or cooks or mothers. Young boys playing with their slings and catapults, young girls fetching water from the nearby spring, older women sitting beside a fire made of thorn bushes, pots of food warming above.

In the fields below the hilltops the men were also at work. Even at this time of year there were preparations to make. Camels or oxen, usually in pairs, were dragging the ploughs through the hard ground. Sometimes a plough would have both a camel and an ox, causing the yoke to rid unevenly over the two animals, chafing their necks and putting an unfair burden on the lower ox.

Having started late in the morning, they covered only twelve miles on the first day and stopped at the first roadside inn they came to. Mary's spirits fell when she saw it. Joseph, wiser in the world than she was, had warned her not to expect too much but even so she was shocked by the sight of it.

It was designed to do no more than provide overnight shelter and a meal of sorts to whoever should turn up, tourist or trader, government courier or any of the lost souls who seemed to spend their lives on the move. Any rich traveller would avoid such places, finding friends to stay with; any government official travelling on important business would automatically be put up with the town mayor or magistrate.

Mary found herself shepherded into a small barely furnished room with Zara and two other women. There were two tiny bedsteads and two sleeping mats on the floor. There was one candleholder and one chamber pot, no seats and nowhere to put clothing or goods.

The animals had been left outside in a muddy courtyard and Mary could only hope that Herod's rule of law extended to this particular spot and the donkey would still be there in the morning.

Mary had also been warned by Joseph that they were at the mercy of the owners, not famous for their honesty or fair dealing and likely to ask outrageous sums of money for very little hospitality. The food provided was uninviting and minimal; the washing facilities nothing more than an outhouse beside the well with no privacy to speak of. By the time morning came she was desperate to get away and couldn't help wondering what sort of madcap idea this journey was.

But they did better the next time, for one of the party had a friend with a large establishment some twenty miles further on. Here they managed to bed themselves down in a draughty but relatively clean barn, well protected from the easterly wind and with the strange but comforting benefit of the backs of cows to warm themselves against as they slept.

Two days later they reached the point where the party was to split up. All but one other woman, Esther, were going to Jerusalem. Mary said a sad goodbye to Zara but was grateful that Esther was continuing in her own direction, past Hebron down to Beersheba. How she would manage alone after Mary had arrived at Hebron she couldn't imagine, but Esther was older and tougher and well-travelled and seemed not to be worrying in the least about the journey.

As they left the route to Jerusalem behind them and began their slow way along a far rougher road, Mary began to realise what a fount of knowledge Esther was.

"Look ahead," Esther exclaimed, pointing towards the horizon. Mary looked and found herself staring at an astonishing sight, a great round fortification built on a mountain top.

"It's the Herodium," said Esther, "Herod's palace-cum-tomb-cum-castle, built on the site of one of his great victories. And look - see that other mountain - the flat-topped one next to it? They were once a pair, the "twin-breasted mountains" they used to call them. But he lopped the top off one and placed it on the other so nothing could be higher than his castle."

They walked on past the tiny village of Beit Sahur. Visible even from the road were the flowing robes of the last few shepherds still up on the hills despite the cold. Almost frozen herself, Mary shivered at the thought of the life they must lead, unprotected against both bandits and weather.

Soon they found themselves skirting whole banks of olive groves stretching upwards towards a little town on the hillside above them.

"What's that up there?" asked Mary as they walked below it.

"That's Bethlehem, the House of Bread. Or the Arabs call it Beit Lahm, meaning the House of Flesh. In both cases it means a good town, plentiful with supplies. In the scriptures it is referred to as Bethlehem

Ephrathah or Bethlehem Judah, where the Messiah is supposed to be going to be born."

Mary's thorough knowledge of the scriptures had let her down for a moment. She knew the reference when Esther made it. But the precise words made her jump. She had completely overlooked the connection between Joseph's family and the town mentioned by Micah in his writings. She was careful in her reply.

"Bethlehem," she repeated thoughtfully, "that's where my future husband's family came from. He is of the line of David, perhaps twenty-eight generations on. I wonder if we shall ever go there."

As they moved slowly on they came upon a pillar set above a small stone tomb by the wayside. Mary looked across questioningly at Esther, by now expecting her to know everything.

"Rachel's tomb," said Esther. "You know the story?"

"Well..." said Mary. She did know, but so enjoyed Esther's lectures she thought she'd like to hear it again. Judging by what she'd learned from Esther so far, there was likely to be more to the story than she already knew.

"It's the story of Rachel and Jacob. Jacob's uncle, Laban, had two children, Leah and Rachel. Jacob loved Rachel and promised his uncle he would work for him for seven years to earn the right to marry her. He worked his seven years but when it came to the wedding he found that Laban had played a trick on him. Instead of finding himself marrying Rachel it was Leah under the veil. Laban had substituted Leah because he didn't want his younger daughter to be married first. There was nothing to be done about it; the marriage ceremony was over and Leah was Jacob's wife. She bore Jacob several children, but really he still loved Rachel and worked another seven years to have her as his second wife. But though they loved each passionately there was sadness at first too, for it was many years before they had their first child, Joseph. They were blissfully happy after that and then Rachel conceived again - but this time she died in childbirth with Benjamin on this very spot. Jacob was heartbroken and built the grave with its pillar here in everlasting memory. The prophet Jeremiah said, 'In Rama (which is very near here) was there a voice heard, lamentation and weeping and great mourning, Rachel weeping for her children and would not be comforted'. The story was that she was weeping for the children of her first son Joseph, who were later to be exiled from their country."

"And what happened to Jacob after she died?"

"He still had Leah, of course, and now they are buried together in the mosque in Hebron, where you are going."

Mary walked on quietly after this, thinking over the sad story and remembering again her own dream. It was strange that the name Joseph had cropped up again. And like any future mother she could not help wondering whether she too might suffer sadness and misery for her children. She thought that that must be the saddest experience of all.

Shortly after Rachel's tomb the road forked; right to Hebron and left to Bethlehem. Mary could not have guessed that in less than nine month's time she would be back, taking the Bethlehem turning, heavily pregnant, just as Rachel had been.

They arrived in Hebron a day later and Mary said a sad farewell to Esther. She had come to admire her deeply, for of all the people she had ever met she seemed the most comfortable within herself; she had an inner serenity and a wide knowledge that combined to give her immense strength and confidence. Mary felt that she would like Esther to be a model for herself and resolved to remember what she had learned from her in those two days of travel.

As she entered her cousin Elizabeth's home she thought at first that there was no one in. She had not managed to get a message to Elizabeth; she had not found anyone going any faster than she herself, so she was not quite sure what to expect. The cousins had not met since Anna and Joachim and she had left Jerusalem and moved north to Nazareth, although they had sent messages to each other from time to time.

She peered through the gloom of the tiny room, overlooked back and front by other dwellings and called out her cousin's name. "Elizabeth? It's me, Mary."

Then as her eyes grew accustomed to the darknesss she could make out the form of Elizabeth asleep. Gently she touched her and said again, "Elizabeth - it's Mary".

Elizabeth sat up, stared in amazement at her cousin and then clutched at her own stomach.

"It moved," she said, "the baby moved. The first time." Such was her excitement she hadn't even welcomed Mary.

Then the two cousins embraced and greeted each other.

"Let me look at you Mary, it's been so long." The older woman drew back and stared hard at Mary's face.

"What?" said Mary, feeling there was something behind the questioning look.

"Nothing," said Elizabeth, "it's just so good to see you again."

"This is wonderful," said Mary, her arm around Elizabeth, "come on, let's sit and you tell me all about it."

"No, you must first have some refreshment," said Elizabeth, busying herself with some fruit juice, "anyway, tell me about the journey. How did you arrange it?"

"No," said Mary in turn, "my journey is nothing compared with yours."

"Well..." Elizabeth didn't need much encouragement, and she spelt out the joy and excitement of finding out after so many years that she was pregnant at last.

"I truly believed," she said, "that I must have done something terribly wrong for God to deny us a child. For it could not be Zacharias. A priest at the temple...he would do no wrong in God's eyes."

"I cannot believe it was you," said Mary. "Some women go for ages without conceiving. It's surely nothing more than that."

"But I am fifty-five," said Elizabeth, "this must be a miracle of some sort. In fact..." Her voice tailed off, as she seemed to wonder how to continue.

Mary went over to sit beside her, feeling there was something more behind Elizabeth's uncertainty. She put her arm around her cousin and said simply, "Yes?"

"Oh Mary," said Elizabeth, "I have to tell someone and I cannot think of anyone better than you. I - we - have kept it to ourselves for so long, yet it's so amazing."

"Tell me," said Mary encouragingly, getting up and giving Elizabeth a goblet of juice to fortify her.

"It's so hard to believe, yet now we have the proof." And Elizabeth patted her stomach gently and smiled at Mary. "It was Zacharias. He was burning incense in the temple and the congregation were praying when he had a vision. I tell you Mary, the angel Gabriel appeared to him. He was standing right next to the altar and spoke to him!"

Mary clutched Elizabeth again, her arm around her, for she could see that Elizabeth was feeling faint, though whether it was at the memory or through her condition she was unable to tell.

"Are you sure? Could it not just be that being in the temple, and with the strong smell of the incense..."

But Elizabeth stopped her. "No, it really happened. Zacharias was terrified, as you might imagine. He couldn't believe it either. But he has suffered for not believing, I can tell you. Then the angel spoke, and do you know what he said, Mary? He said that our prayers had been heard and that we should have a son. We're going to call him John."

Immediately Mary recognised the echo of her own dream. To distract herself from the puzzling thought she tried to continue talking normally. "But there's never been a John in the family - it's not a family name at all," said Mary, not at all sure how much of this made sense.

"The angel told us: 'You must call him John' ".

"But it's wonderful," Mary said, leaving the subject of the name, "and now it's proven. You see, God was not punishing you - just making you wait a while."

"But that's not all. Nothing like all."

"Go on." Mary had given up wondering whether to believe it all and decided to allow Elizabeth to tell the whole story. The time for wondering could come later.

But now Elizabeth seemed to grow shy. For a while she said nothing, occasionally looking up at Mary but looking away as soon as she met her eyes.

"Go on," Mary said again, puzzled at the silence.

"Oh Mary." Elizabeth got up and prowled around the little room. "We've never told anyone this, it seems too...unbelievable. He told Zacharias that our baby will be great in the eyes of God. That he shall be full of the Holy Spirit. That he will lead the children of Israel to God. That he will prepare the people for the Messiah! I think it means that our baby, our John, will be a great prophet!"

Mary was dazed to hear this, for inevitably it took her mind back to the memory of her own dream. Could the young man who talked to her have been the same? The angel Gabriel? She was staggered at how the two stories connected - Elizabeth's son preparing the way for the Messiah; Mary herself bearing the Son of God. She felt suddenly scared and it must have shown, for she saw Elizabeth staring at her.

While she was trying to take all this in, a footfall from the doorway made her turn round. Standing framed with the sunlight behind him was Elizabeth's husband and Mary's godfather, the old priest Zacharias.

Silently he approached her and embraced her. Mary started to congratulate him but stopped short as she suddenly realised there was something strange about him. Instead of saying her name and welcoming her to his house as would have been usual, he was doing nothing but smiling and bowing slightly. He kissed her on both cheeks but made no attempt to speak.

"Zacharias...?" she said tentatively, but still getting no response turned back to Elizabeth.

Elizabeth said quietly, "You remember I said Zacharias has suffered for not believing? It was hardly surprising of him - would you have believed what Gabriel said? Zacharias said to Gabriel, 'How can I believe it? I'm an old man and my wife is past childbearing. We can't have children now.' But he was wrong to say that. Wrong to argue." She turned towards Zacharias and in a gesture of solidarity put her arms around him. "Although I would have said the same. But Gabriel made him pay - Zacharias has not spoken a word since then. And the congregation must have realised that something had happened, for they had waited all the time in silence until he came out of the temple, and when he could only beckon to them instead of speaking they knew he had had a vision."

Mary looked from one to the other in bewilderment. They looked back, not surprised that she seemed astonished. But they would have been even more astonished had they realised what she was actually thinking.

She was wondering whether she should tell them about her own vision. For she had at last begun to believe in it. And she was not feeling very well. Especially in the mornings.

CHAPTER 5

THE SHEPHERDS

In Beit Sahur, one of the tiny settlements Mary had glimpsed on her journey to Hebron and one mile to the east of Bethlehem (or Bethlehem as it came to be known) four shepherds were huddled around a fire and one of them had a meaningful leer on his face.

"Stephanos," said Misael the leader, "I think you're about to pull one of your tricks. Something tells me."

Stephanos put an innocent look on his large baby face and pulled his head veil down a bit. "Wind's getting up," he observed.

"Yes, well, come on, what's it about?"

"Why should it be about anything? Can't I have a bit of a think without someone asking what it's all about?"

Acheel snorted. "The day you've got nothing on your mind is the day we'll be burying you. Misael's right. Isn't he Cyriacus? What's the game?"

Cyriacus kept quiet and huddled his thin body deep into his old father's tired camel hair cloak. It didn't take much to unnerve him, and if Stephanos was up to one of his games again he didn't want to know. He could remember the last one only too clearly. It had seemed a very smart idea at the time and in the way Stephanos had outlined it. After all, who was to know if they were running two sets of flocks at the same time? With a bit of planning it wasn't difficult for them to share out their territories and their responsibilities. Being in two places at once was quite easy to achieve when there are four of you, all knowing the job backwards, all light on your feet, all able to cover the ground without difficulty.

But it was too small a community and someone had noticed eventually and it had been a long time before any of the four of them were welcome in Bethlehem again - and that was despite Misael's reputation as an exceptionally reliable lead shepherd who could be trusted with anyone's flock.

Stephanos felt injured. He was only trying to make them all a bit of money, and the Lord above knew they all needed it. Especially Misael himself, the only married one, with three children and an over-large wife to support. Fat lot of thanks you get. Stephanos shrugged his shoulders. Misael might like to remember that the other three had to cover for him when he felt the need to get home and see the family.

"I've just had an idea, that's all. No need to get so excited. It's perfectly honest."

Cyriacus pulled his veil right over his head. If Stephanos claimed it was perfectly honest, that was the time to get really worried.

Misael looked at Stephanos consideringly. Sometimes it was best to ignore it when he was getting one of his ideas. As often as not it went away again before it ever came to anything. But on other occasions, especially when it involved the four of them, it was wiser to investigate a little before they were all sucked into it. And Stephanos's face was betraying excitement; from experience Misael started to worry.

"You'd better tell us Stephanos. I take it it involves us all."

"Well, don't you want a bit of extra income? It's been a very dry year."

They didn't need reminding. Last year's dry summer was already looking as though it were going to repeat itself. If it went on like this things would start to go wrong in a big way. Reduced crops, shortage of grain - and, most important as far as they were concerned, little grazing. It was hard enough keeping hold of their patches of land for the flocks entrusted to them. But when the grass was brown instead of green and the streams dried up it was hard being a shepherd. The flocks were down in number and income sank to match. Stephanos was right, of course. But then, when couldn't they all do with extra money?

The other three considered quietly

It was all very well, Acheel thought to himself, for Misael to claim we're the latest in a line of great tradition as he so often did. Yes: Abraham, Isaac, Jacob; they were all shepherds, all great men from Jewish history. But try telling that to your stomach. There didn't seem much glory in being so hungry you got cold even on a warm summer's evening from sheer lack of fat to cover your bones. He got out a few raisins and munched ruminatively.

"Go on," said Misael. They had better know the worst.

"What year is it?" asked Stephanos by way of reply.

Acheel the intellectual started to calculate but was interrupted by Misael's raised hand. He had heard something.

"Listen..."

They listened. Within seconds they had all heard it. Misael's famed professional ear had once again proved itself. It was distant and it was muffled. But they all knew what it was.

"Come on," said Misael. "We'll get them into the fold first. We've got time for that."

The four of them spread out, each making their own sounds: Cyriacus and Acheel their strange, half-cooing, half-speech noises, Misael and Stephanos whistling. Each went in a different direction, each calling their own flocks to them. Quickly the little baas and bleats showed the sheep were responding and within a very few minutes each was leading his flock to the sheepfold; the high mortarless walled enclosure where they were safe from the bears and jackals that were the shepherds' permanent enemy.

"Cyriacus - you stay," said Misael.

Cyriacus nodded. "The Lord preserve you," he said and settled himself in the open gateway to the enclosure, the sheep safely inside.

"I'm sure he will," said Acheel drily.

The three of them took up their staffs and rope and set off in the direction of the sound that Misael had heard.

The ground quickly led from pasture to a rocky slope, edging a valley. From low down they heard the unmistakeable bleat of the lost sheep, perhaps fifty yards down the steep slope, wedged into a rocky crevice.

"See anything?" asked Acheel of Misael, who was automatically in the lead and peering down the side of the slope.

"Not a thing." Misael held out his hand for Acheel to take and leaned dangerously out and peered downwards. "Ah yes... Stupid animal..." He pulled himself up again and looked around. "Tie it there." He started to point but Stephanos was ahead of him and had already started for the tree to tie the rope around.

With Acheel steadying it and Stephanos keeping an eye on his knots, Misael began lowering himself down the incline, kicking against the side with his rope-based boots and cursing to himself as the jagged edges pushed through the unforgiving soles. After about twenty yards the slope got easier and Misael was able to slip himself out of the rope. "Relax a minute," he called up.

He could see the sheep now, only about thirty yards away and down to the left. It stood, as they so often did, waiting for help, impassive yet also looking faintly offended that anyone should have allowed this to happen to him. At first sight it was unharmed, but the continual bleating told Misael that something was wrong. As he stared he saw it was standing with one back leg slightly askew. It would have been surprising had there not been some injury; no sheep could fall fifty feet and escape without hurt. With luck it would only be a bruise, but if it was a break it probably meant the end. Misael cursed; with things as they were losing even one sheep was bad news.

"OK there. Hang on." He scrambled the last few yards, whistling encouragement as he went; it was one of his own flock and it would take comfort from the sound of its friend and master. On the other hand, when it came to the lift it was a pity it wasn't Acheel's or Stephanos's. At this time of year they were still lambs, destined for sacrifice at the temple, and considerably lighter than his own sheep, used for spinning wool and later for sheepskin coats.

Acheel was peering over the top; he could see where Misael had got to and called back to Stephanos: "He's got there." And in answer to the unspoken question, "Can't tell yet."

Misael put his hand on the sheep's back. It had stopped bleating and was now staring pathetically straight at him. Despite himself and the predicament, Misael smiled. Stupid they were and not particularly friendly - but there was something about sheep that simply got beneath his skin. He couldn't envisage any other lifestyle. It was unbearably cold in the winter and unbearably hot in the summer. Living outdoors in open caves provided few home comforts. There was little to eat; there were predators and thieves to guard against; there was either a shortage of water or a flood. And being married provided the additional worries of not being able to provide enough money and barely seeing the family grow up.

He felt the leg. The sheep was irritable and showed it. It made a vague attempt to escape from his hands, pawing back and forth. Misael treated it with care. It might be grateful to see him and to be rescued, but a sick sheep was a dangerous sheep. It had plenty of body weight and if it decided to lean on you or tread on your foot or even butt you with its head you knew all about it.

"All right, all right," said Misael soothingly, cautiously standing to one side as he examined the damaged leg. He thought it was probably not broken. Deliberately he squeezed it, alert to the danger of being kicked. The sheep reared a little, uttered a noise somewhere between a bleat and a swear word, and put the foot down again. Satisfied with his diagnosis that it was nothing more than bruising Misael looked up. He could just see Acheel craning down at him.

"Just bruising I think. I'll try to get it up," he called.

Misael looked again at the sheep. It appeared to have calmed down now he had stopped touching the leg. It was making no sound but simply staring impassively ahead, waiting.

Misael knew was what in front of him and took a deep breath. He was a strong man, the biggest and strongest of all of them, but the oldest too. It would take all that strength to do what he had to do.

He sank to his knees and made his comforting whistling sound. The sheep turned its head slightly towards him, as if to say, "OK, I understand, let's get on with it. I'll try and be good."

Misael slipped his arms around the front and back legs and tentatively pushed his head beneath its stomach. The sheep seemed to be ignoring him; a good sign. Misael wriggled forward until his head was out the other side and braced himself to begin to stand. The sheep was heavy; a dead weight that offered no help. For a moment Misael wondered if he could do it and whether he should get Acheel to come down too. But having got thus far he decided to try. Balancing himself carefully he punished his leg and thigh muscles by pushing them apart as he clambered and wobbled to his feet. The sheep was still ignoring him despite the ignominious position it was in. Misael accepted this without thought; it was no more than an acknowledgment of the close-knit life they led that a wild animal would allow this to happen.

Now standing fully vertical Misael started the climb upwards. For the first thirty yards it was hard but straightforward. The leg muscles were crying and the heart was straining, but Misael was able to keep moving.

Then came the final, much more difficult, twenty yards; far more vertical and needing the rope for assistance. But while Misael was considering how best to go about it he realised that Acheel was coming down. As so often, knowing each other so well, there was no need for speech between them. Acheel had anticipated the difficulties and was on his way to help. He had brought his staff with him and Misael could see what was in his mind.

When down next to Misael, Acheel barely spoke. He slipped himself from the rope and tied it carefully round Misael. He jerked his head, as though to say "Get going", and positioned himself to Misael's side. Misael realised why it was Acheel and not Stephanos who had come down. Nimble and by far the best climber among them, Acheel seemed to have the ability to move up and down any rock face, whether it had footholds or not. In parallel they started to move slowly upwards, Misael allowing Stephanos above to help him by pulling at the rope, Acheel ascending below and just to one side of him and holding the sheep's head away from the cliff side with the curved top of his staff. It was a procedure they had accomplished many times before.

But it was hard. Simply raising the weight of the sheep fifty yards made colossal demands on Misael and he was quickly fighting for breath while at the same time having to search for footholds. Acheel could tell that the strain on his back and neck was becoming intolerable and he moved up across and behind him, somehow finding a spare hand to put beneath the sheep and take some of the weight.

And thus they finished the climb; like two crabs linked together, moving agonising slowly and sideways up the cliff face until eventually the three heads appeared over the edge to be greeted by Stephanos's large face grinning back. The good shepherds had done it many times before, but each time was a still a triumph.

Two hours later, as dusk began to fall, they each took a walk around their flocks and then came together in the low rock-walled encampment for their supper. Cyriacus had gathered enough wood to build up the fire. Even though it was late spring the nights were cold and they crouched close.

Their provisions didn't amount to very much. They only had what they could carry up from the town. Just about enough bread, cheese, olives, figs, dates and raisins to carry them through till one of them went down to Bethlehem again some time the following day. To drink, nothing but cold clean water from the nearby spring.

The sheep appeared to have recovered from its adventure. It wasn't walking about much, and still stood with its back foot at a slightly odd angle, but Misael was reasonably sure there was nothing seriously wrong.

Stephanos coughed; an attention-seeking cough.

"Oh no," said Acheel.

"Well," said Stephanos, "it was a good idea before, it's still a good idea."

They had all hoped he'd forgotten his latest plan during the sheep episode, whatever it was. But he was not so easily diverted.

"I was asking what the date was. Acheel?"

Acheel shook his head. Dates didn't mean much.

"All right," said Stephanos, "let's put it another way. What happens every fourteen years - and hasn't happened for thirteen and a half?"

Misael knew. "The census."

This woke Acheel up properly. "The census. The excuse for Quirinius to take even more money from us."

Misael said, "You can't blame Quirinius, much as you might want to. To start with, it's his first term as Governor of Syria, and anyway, he only does what the Emperor Caesar Augustus tells him."

"Well why doesn't Herod do something about it?" asked Acheel, querulous as ever when it came to politics. "He's supposed to be King of the Jews, even if he isn't one himself. Why doesn't he stand up for us?"

"He's sort of a Jew," said Cyriacus, sensing an argument and trying to head it off.

"Not even sort of, he's an Arab," said Acheel scornfully. "Both his parents were Arabs. He's from Idumea. And don't forget, he's officially a Roman, thanks to his father's friendship with Julius Caesar. It's all wheels within wheels. Otherwise why would Caesar Augustus make him King of Judaea?"

"Herod's wife was a Jewish princess." Cyriacus was not quite giving up.

"His second wife. The lovely Mariamne. But the first one wasn't, not Dorish. He only divorced her to further his career. Anyway, look what happened to Mariamne. Put to death because he didn't trust her. Herod's not a Jew, he's a mad murderer." Acheel was in full flood. He had stopped eating and was giving a good imitation of being one of the politicians he so detested.

"Well it's just as well there aren't any Romans up here to hear all that or I wouldn't give much for your chances. Anyway," said Misael, who was getting a little tired of this and didn't appreciate arguments at nightfall, "there's no point in expecting Herod to do anything about it. If the Emperor Augustus wants a census - yes, and I know it's all to do with raising money - he'll have a census. And no amount of moaning is going to stop it."

"Right," said Stephanos, wanting to get on with his own agenda. "So there'll be a census, like it or not. What does that tell you?"

"That the great Roman Empire is short of money?" Acheel had started eating again but was still in argumentative mood.

"It tells us," Stephanos said triumphantly, with all the pride of a man who is about to reveal the future, "that there will be a lot of people descending on Bethlehem."

"Won't be able to move," muttered Acheel, still irritated.

"It tells us," Stephanos repeated, "that there will be a lot of business in the town. And it tells us they'll want somewhere to stay."

"There's the caravansary," said Acheel, still grumpily not wanting to agree with anyone.

"Oh, yes," said Stephanos, "and when did anyone get in there when it's busy? Anyway you've got to pay the price. And it's two miles out of town. We're not all merchants or travellers."

Their conversation was interrupted by a jackal call. Misael sat up, listening. They all stopped talking and Cyriacus grabbed at his sling-shot. They waited in silence but the call was already sounding farther off and they settled down again, Stephanos heaving some more wood on the fire.

"So?" Misael, though bored with Stephanos's little plots, thought they'd better get it out into the open and, with a bit of luck, out of the way.

"So..." said Stephanos, the grin back on his moon face and sounding like a magician about to pull off his latest trick, "...who can help them find somewhere to stay? Who knows people in Bethlehem with room to spare, even if it's only under the house? Who knows all the habitable caves around here?"

"Tell me," sighed Acheel.

"We do," said Steph triumphantly.

"Yes?" Cyriacus sounded alarmed. He didn't much like meeting strangers and this was beginning to sound suspiciously as though that was exactly what Stephanos's scheme might mean.

"So...who better to act as accommodation guides and pocket some cash at the same time? We can get a bit from the travellers and another bit from the houseowners. And when they run out, we can show them to the caves, which we will have tidied up a bit, and charge rental. How about that?" Stephanos's face, shining brightly in the rising moon, was suffused with his grin.

There was a moment's silence, before Misael reluctantly said, "It's not a bad idea, I must say."

"Three of us, or even two, can guard the flocks – using the fold – while the others carry out the business." Even Acheel seemed quite enthusiastic. And Stephanos was right, there was nothing exactly illegal about it.

Cyriacus began to enter into the spirit of the idea. "We could use Nigdal Eder too."

"We could," said Misael. Nigdal Eder was a tower on the road to Jerusalem used by many of the other shepherds around there to keep an overall watch on their flocks. They themselves didn't tend to use it much, preferring to cover the ground on foot. "Provided they don't ask why we've taken a sudden interest in it."

Cyriacus had a new thought, though one that was never far from his mind. "And it'll be a good test too, a good preparation."

"Preparation?" Misael looked questioningly at Cyriacus.

"You know. For when the Messiah comes."

"Oh...!" Acheel's irritation had returned. "Not that again."

"You know what the prophet says: 'But thou, Bethlehem Ephratah, though thou shall be little among the thousands of Judah, yet out of thee shall He come forth unto me that is to be ruler in Israel'." Cyriacus, the religious one, was word perfect, as ever.

"Yes, all right. But why now? It needn't be for a thousand years."

"Have faith my friend. The Messiah will come. And we must be ready."

Stephanos saw his chance. "Absolutely right, Cyriacus. Let's be ready. So - who's for my plan? Who wants to make some money?"

Misael nodded. He started to gather some rushes from the pile and lay them within a little circle of stones to make his bed. He had to admit, it was one of Stephanos's better suggestions.

CHAPTER 6

JOSEPH

In Hebron Mary had decided she could only stay with Elizabeth for about three months. She would love to have stayed until the baby was born - the baby boy who was to be called John, if she was to believe in the vision which Zacharias claimed to have seen in the temple.

But she worried about her parents and felt she could leave them no longer. She was also beginning to miss Joseph, although in the back of her mind she knew there would great difficulty when they met again. But most of all she wanted to get the journey done before the pregnancy took her over.

Mary was a quiet and logical girl, who while being a good Jew was not disposed to believe in the magic of visions and ghosts. Privately she believed that Zacharias had suffered no more than a temporary blackout, probably brought on by an extra strong dose of incense in the thurible as he swung it about. She had no knowledge of how the mind worked but suspected that the dumbness which he seemed to be afflicted with was no more than an effect of the little stroke and would pass in time.

Over the following weeks she and Elizabeth worked easily together, Mary automatically taking over some of the heavier tasks as Elizabeth's pregnancy became more obvious. Also her cousin seemed rather sheepish about being pregnant at her age, and tried as hard as she could to stay out of the public view, so Mary it was who paid regular visits to the market for provisions and went to and fro to the well for water.

Together they carried on the usual family tasks: baking the bread, making curds from goat's milk, spinning and weaving - especially necessary as Elizabeth grew in size and needed new robes and there would soon be a baby in the family for the first time, with all the clothing that would require.

Life was not easy, and with Zacharias old and still unable to speak, Elizabeth was grateful for the presence of her cousin, who provided what women need in pregnancy: someone of their own sex to talk things over with, share in the changes that were taking place in the body, plan and prepare for the future.

But while Mary spent her time supporting her older cousin she was wrestling with her own problem. For she could no longer pretend to herself. And she knew that sooner or later Elizabeth would say something. She had already caught her cousin looking at her speculatively and knew what she was wondering.

In the end she was caught out. Lifting the heavy goatskin bucket full of water and thinking she was alone she gave a groan and arched her back as women have done from time immemorial as their time moved on.

But Elizabeth had come into the room unheard.

She said simply, "Mary?"

Mary turned and looked at her and smiled helplessly.

Elizabeth again said simply, "You too." It was a statement, not a question.

Mary set the bucket down and lowered herself to the ground. She made the slight groan again, astonished at how grateful she was she no longer had to pretend.

Elizabeth, far advanced in pregnancy, lowered herself more carefully and sat beside her cousin. It was, thought Mary, rather comic, two portly ladies settled down on the floor next to each other like a pair of skittles.

As they leaned against the wall, Elizabeth put her hand out to Mary but said nothing. She waited for Mary to say whatever she wanted to say.

Mary for her part knew she had to commit herself to something. All these weeks she had known what was happening to her, yet did not understand why. Reluctant as she had always been to accept any truth from that dream she was still teetering between belief and disbelief. But now she was grateful for one thing; at last there was someone to share it with. The decision had been taken for her.

"Yes, me too," she said finally. "Although I don't know how."

Elizabeth looked a little puzzled. "But you are betrothed to Joseph. It is not uncommon during betrothal. To all intents and purposes you are married - the child will be legitimate. You are already called husband and wife. It's only that you don't move from your house to his until the ceremony."

"But we haven't..." Mary stopped short. It was too private, even for two pregnant cousins who had lived and worked together for the last month.

But however surprised Elizabeth was she seemed to understand, for she said gently, "You can still be a virgin and pregnant. It can happen. Perhaps you have lain close together..." She didn't go on. She thought Mary could work out the rest for herself.

Mary's mind was in turmoil. While turning over what Elizabeth had suggested she decided she must tell the rest of the story and made the decision to tell her about her dream and what the young man had said.

If Mary had thought ahead she would have realised what Elizabeth's reaction would be. Believing her husband had himself received a messenger from God, Elizabeth had no problem in believing Mary had had the same.

Elizabeth's response was immediate and positive and full of faith: "How blessed you are! And so is the child in your womb!" She found herself crying tears of joy and clutched Mary so hard that Mary worried about both their babies. "Of course, now it all makes sense. Remember what the prophet Isiah said: 'A virgin would conceive a son who would be named Immanuel - God is with us'." Whether Mary was pregnant by Joseph or by an act of God no-one would ever know, but to Elizabeth everything made sense.

Now she knew it was no coincidence that her child had moved in the womb for the first time when Mary arrived. How could the child do otherwise when the mother of the Messiah arrived? When the mother of the man her son John was to prepare the way for arrived in their tiny home?

If she felt incredulous that such honour was being bestowed on two lowly women living humdrum lives in small towns in Israel she quickly subdued the feeling. She felt humble that they should have been chosen, but at the same time believed it was God's way to work through the poor not the rich.

Still holding the silently crying Elizabeth in her arms, Mary felt that she was indeed blessed. She still could not bring herself to believe totally that she was to bear the Son of God; that was surely impossible. But there was something special about her child... (If the thought occurred to her that that was what every mother said, she put it conveniently to the back of her mind.)

Eventually Mary found herself speaking. As any devout Jew would she automatically praised the Lord for his gift of a child.

"Yes, Elizabeth, you are right. I am blessed - everyone will call me blessed. I thank the Lord for the great gift he has bestowed on me despite my lowly state. He is merciful to the poor and the weak but not to the proud. He looks after the hungry but makes the rich look after themselves. And he has protected our country Israel and all its sons and daughters from Abraham onwards."

Mary was not used to making speeches and found herself surprised at her own eloquence. But she was so steeped in the scriptures that somehow the words had come out naturally. If Elizabeth was a little taken aback at her cousin's language she said nothing but continued to hold her tightly. In Elizabeth's mind there was no uncertainty; if the Lord's messenger had appeared to Mary in a dream and told her she was to bear the Son of God, that was exactly what was to happen. The two of them were the most honoured people in the world. If it was a monumental thought, it was also a simple one. And Elizabeth was happy to believe it.

Soon Mary started looking out for someone to travel homewards with. Eventually finding a small caravan which was going north she said her goodbyes to Elizabeth and Zacharias and set off homewards.

She began the journey full of dread. Despite Elizabeth's conviction that she was indeed bearing the Son of God in her womb, Mary also knew how it would seem to Joseph. She could not get the sight of the woman on the Synagogue steps out of her mind and the sound of the crowd baying for her death. Mary's only comfort was to hope that if Elizabeth was right, then surely God would come to her rescue in some way.

As the outskirts of Nazareth came into view Mary felt her heart thumping. Now more than a third of the way through her pregnancy it was going to be impossible to disguise it from Joseph. Her loose robes did not make it obvious, but as soon as she would spend a little time with him he was sure to notice.

She hardly knew what to say to him. She didn't feel he would be very ready to believe the story of her dream and the man's astonishing announcement, despite the fact that Elizabeth had immediately seen the connection between her own situation and Mary's. She was also not too sure about Elizabeth's other suggestion, that it was possible to be both virgin and pregnant. It was a delicate matter to talk about, despite their closeness. And the memory of the woman at the synagogue steps kept coming back to haunt her.

It was a day or so before Joseph noticed.

When he did, he said nothing, but simply stared at her. Unsure how to respond, Mary looked back, the stricken look on her face expressing her feelings. Unfortunately for her, Joseph interpreted the look as one of guilt rather than worry and turned and walked away without speaking.

She called after him, "Joseph…"

But he ignored her and continued walking away.

She ran after him, calling. "Please, let me talk to you…there is something I must tell you…"

Her words were not very well chosen, for again he misinterpreted them. The automatic thought that was in his mind was, naturally enough, that she had been unfaithful to him.

She stopped running, out of breath with the exertion and the natural inhibiting effect of the child she was carrying, and watched him hurrying away, head down.

Joseph unconsciously repeated Mary's own actions when she rushed from the stoning at the synagogue. He climbed far up onto the mountain, so that he too could see the Sea of Galilee spread out below him. It was now early April, well into the lambing season. He could hear nothing but the bleating of the sheep and their newborn offspring, now released from their winter quarters and back on the hills.

He could not believe what he had seen. Mary of all people. Mary, the God-loving, God-fearing, pure sixteen-year-old that his parents had matched with him only six months earlier and who he had been so thrilled to become betrothed to after the dreadful loss of his first wife.

His first thought was that it must have been someone she had met while in Hebron, though he wasn't certain that there had been time enough for the baby to begin to show. He felt a violent rage well up in him, first against Mary, then against the man, whoever he was. Or what about that Roman soldier he had seen looking at her more than once? He was a good-looking young man and those Romans had a way with them, to say nothing of the power they wielded. Or then again perhaps she had been raped. That was entirely possible on that journey. Perhaps if it had happened as she travelled to Hebron, it would be showing by now. Perhaps that was what she wanted to tell him. But he quickly talked himself out of that; if something like that had happened she would have told him immediately. Or would she? Perhaps she was too ashamed. Perhaps he had been far too abrupt in rushing off. But then, none of that mattered. She was bearing a child and it was not his and the only thing left to him to do was divorce her. There was no need for another stoning; it was not his style. Divorce was easy and quite enough. Just write a letter, fix it up at the synagogue and the engagement was over.

He didn't want to make a spectacle of her. He did not have to give a reason. She could simply go away somewhere to have the baby and no-one would be any the wiser. Yes. That was the way to do it. Not cause her any more embarrassment than he had to. There was no need for that. But there must be a divorce. He already had two children of his own; he didn't need one of someone else's as well.

The argument raged back and forth in his mind. After an hour of worry and decision and counter-decision he was tired and lay back on the ground in the shelter of a large rock.

Perhaps he had a dream while he was asleep. Perhaps a visitation. When he awoke he could remember nothing, but his mind was filled with a completely new idea.

He had always believed Mary to be the purest of people and he still wanted to believe it. Something was telling him to rise above the problem. A new life was beginning, and whatever the fault - or not - of the mother, it was certainly not the fault of the child. A new baby was always pure and deserved the best of treatment. Every new child was a child of God, and therefore so was the child in Mary's womb.

Whatever had happened, the more he thought the more he simply couldn't believe that Mary had been deliberately unfaithful. Therefore whatever had happened she was not to blame, and it was his duty, as a human being, a Jew, a descendent of the great line of David, to take and protect this new life born to his betrothed.

As with every newborn baby, God is with us, he thought.

And went back to Mary.

Back in Hebron, Elizabeth's time soon came and, as was predicted, she bore a son. Her friends gave thanks to God that despite her age she was safely delivered, with a child that was perfect in every way.

Eight days later Elizabeth and Zacharias went to have the child circumcised. Their friends immediately began to call the boy Zacharias after his father, but Elizabeth stopped them, telling them he was to be called John.

"But it's not a family name," objected one of the women in the congregation, "ask Zacharias himself".

So they asked Zacharias, still unable to speak for himself, to make signs. He indicated he wanted a writing tablet and when it was brought, wrote simply, "His name is John".

The small crowd were puzzled but remembering the story of his vision in the temple, knew something strange was in the air. Deciding they should accept what Zacharias had written - for after all he was a priest at the temple and it was his own firstborn son - they sent up their prayers and loudly thanked God for the safe delivery of the new child John.

They could not have guessed at the effect all this was to have.

For there and then, after nine months, Zacharias suddenly spoke and to their amazement and fear immediately began offering prayers to God: "Blessed be the Lord God, for he has come to see us and protect us against our enemies..."

But it was what he said next that amazed and perplexed them. For he referred to the ancient prophecies that said there would be prophets born of two families who would save their peoples, with the strong hint that one of these would be the Messiah. But it was clear it was not John who was to be the Messiah, for Zacharias added, "And this child John will be the prophet of the Messiah himself. He will show us how to be ready and how to gain salvation by repentance of our sins. He will provide light in the darkness and guide us into peace."

The people around them were silent in amazement and stared at each other, wondering in their hearts about this child John, who their priest said was preparing the way for the Messiah.

Mary and Joseph's wedding day at the beginning of May was hot; perfect for those who were looking forward to celebrating, less than perfect for someone carrying a child. Nevertheless Mary was determined to enjoy the day and gave never-ending thanks for Joseph's decision to go ahead with the marriage.

They had talked it all over and Mary had told him exactly what she had told Elizabeth. She also quoted the prophet Isiah as Elizabeth had. And even then, she - and Joseph - didn't really know what to believe. The idea was simply too big to accept. But Joseph was sure of one thing: he had made the right decision to marry Mary, and no matter what happened in the future he was confident about their partnership.

Many in the little town knew Mary or Joseph or both and a good crowd assembled. Mary had chosen her wedding clothes carefully so that the pregnancy was not too obvious.

Anna, her mother, of course had noticed Mary's condition. Mary had given her the same explanation she had given Elizabeth and Joseph. If Anna found it hard to believe, she didn't say so. She simply decided to herself that they had been together as was perfectly common during betrothal and just made it her business to support her pregnant daughter.

Anna and Joachim, old as they were, had done much to prepare the day. They had dressed themselves up in clothes specially woven for the occasion and beamed with pride and excitement at the sight of their daughter in the elaborate and beautifully embroidered wedding garments she and her friends had handmade for the occasion.

Her female attendants stood waiting at the door of her parents' house, some with the traditional clay oil lamps lighted to ensure the house was bright and cheerful, some swinging small bottles of oil in case the lamps should run out.

When Joseph left his own house, he too had attendants, also carrying lighted torches. Arriving at Joachim's door he proudly rapped upon it and formally asked to see Mary.

When she appeared, the veil drawn across her face, he gently lifted it and as tradition required (though it was not difficult) cried out in delight at what he saw and the treasure that had been given him. Then all the party took up the cry and together they all walked in triumphant procession through the streets and back to Joseph's house for the wedding feast.

Although Joseph did not make a lot of money as a carpenter in a small town and normally lived on the simplest of fare – bread baked from barley instead of wheat, fruit such as figs, dates and pomegranates, the occasional pigeon or fin and scaled fish – he had saved enough to make the feast one to remember. He and his friends had performed the ritual slaughter of one cow and one goat, roasted both and provided enough food for all the guests and several days to come.

Festivities went on for another two days, with dancing, singing, processing, eating, drinking and regular blessings from everyone to everyone.

And when all was over, with Mary and Joseph finally ensconced in the little carpenter's house, they began to look forward to the next celebration. Although at that moment they had no idea that the baby was to be born seventy miles to the south and in a very different environment.

CHAPTER 7

PREPARATION

"Melchior"

"Hormizdah!"

"Jairus, old friend!"

"And Perozadh of Sheba!"

"Hor!"

"...and Yazdegerd – all the way from Saba!"

"Gallio and Lucan!"

The names and the welcomes rang around the ornate room. It was two months after Mary and Joseph's wedding, and away to the east the Magi were congregating in Babylon, preparing themselves for their journey.

In the end there were to be eleven of them, together with servants and camel attendants, led by the three close friends, Melchior (descendent of Shem), Balthazar (of Japheth) and Caspar (of Ham).

The Magi were a deep-rooted sect who could trace their ancestry back many hundreds of years. They were not all well thought of; there were as many charlatans and questionable magicians as there were scientific Magi. The small band who were preparing to set off for the journey west were all Zoroastrian priests and astrologers. Most were genuine scientific seekers after truth; a few were keen to put a history of dubious practice behind them. All would want to show themselves in a good light to any future king who was to be born.

The original Magi had their origins many years before even Zoroaster himself. Born over 600 years earlier, Zoroaster believed he had seen a vision of Ahura Mazda, the Almighty Being, when he was thirty. After managing to convert his king Vishtaspa to his thinking, his teaching spread rapidly through Persia and became its official religion. The Zoroastrian Magi had a reputation for being the most accurate of predictors.

They were used to treks like this one, often spending months of each year on the great caravan routes, travelling mile upon mile in search of different views of the stars and planets, or visiting noblemen and royalty in a dozen different countries to celebrate or foretell the latest great event as seen in the stars.

Babylon was perhaps the most important of the Magi centres. The Babylonians had invaded Jerusalem six hundred years earlier during the time of Nebuchadnezzar and thousands of Jews were taken captive and exiled back to Babylon. Fifty years later Babylon itself was taken by Cyrus the Persian and the Jews were allowed to return to their homeland. But not all went back; many preferred to stay where their new roots had been put down. It was not surprising therefore that the expectation of the Jewish Messiah was strong in Babylon; not surprising that the Magi had for years been anticipating the birth of the new King of the Jews.

Wine began to flow freely; the Magi were not above enjoying themselves. They were used to spending long hours together on their camels and on their overnight rests. There was a strong sense of camaraderie; they enjoyed each others' company and had everything in common. Preparations before a journey always included a few celebrations.

"So where exactly are we going Melchior?" asked Basantor. "The exact town if you please. I know your wanderings - could be taking us anywhere."

"Unfair," cried Melchior. "It only happened the once." This was a reference to an ill-fated journey down the Euphrates which ended in the arrival at a village which had long been deserted and which Melchior had fondly believed was the site of an ancient prophet. All that was to be seen was half a dozen empty caves and the ruins of a small farmhouse. It appeared that Melchior had misread the signs - an indication of his failing eyesight thought Kaeso privately, though he had never felt the need to share this thought.

"I know exactly where we're going," said Melchior strongly, bolstered by the wine. "Straight to Jerusalem."

"Because...?" Yazdegerd was on Basantor's side. It was all light-hearted but there was a touch of realism there too; none of them wanted to spend more time than they had to in the heat of the summer sun which was already beginning to bake the desert land between them and Israel.

"Because if he's to be King of the Jews as all the signs tell us, what better place to start than the capital of Judaea? We can't follow the bright light, if that's what you're thinking - it's already faded and anyway it doesn't move. We know nothing more precise than that it's to do with Israel; we must ask for guidance when we get to the capital."

"Ask who?" demanded Basantor, who had set himself up as chief negotiator on this topic.

"Herod of course, who else?"

"What? Have you thought this through? Do you think one King of the Jews is going to be thrilled about the birth of another one? Not noted for his forbearance, our Herod. I don't think there's going to be room for two kings in his mind."

"It's not the same," objected Perozadh, who felt that Melchior was being unfairly treated here. "To start with Herod's not a Jew at all; he was just put in position to look after the country. And anyway, this child to be born will be a spiritual leader; nothing to do with Herod's position as the Roman's appointed leader."

Basantor was letting the drink get to him. "How do you know that?" he demanded truculently. "The prophecies say there will be a Messiah, come to deliver the Jews from their oppressors. There's nothing spiritual about that. That means war my friend, and to go to war you need a real leader, not a spiritual one. That means a rival for Herod. And that means trouble for everyone, including us, if we're any too near."

Caspar put his tankard down noisily. So far he had let his friend Melchior fight on his own, but now he felt the old man needed a bit of support.

"Shame on you Basantor," he said, "do you not think Melchior has thought about this? Do you really think he'd lead us into trouble?"

"Perhaps we should be thinking of the baby and his parents, not us," said Perozadh, trying to smooth the atmosphere. "You know how proud Herod is. And he's not exactly in control of himself these days, is he?"

Kaeso spoke up. "Perozadh has a point. We all know how he is. Unpredictable, to say the least."

"Whose side are you on, Kaeso?" said Melchior, only just smiling.

Kaeso sensed danger; he hadn't meant to be controversial. But it was true. They all knew how Herod was these days. "Our side, of course," he said, smiling optimistically back. "It's true, isn't it? You can't be sure what Herod's going to do next. Look what he's already done to his own family. And the state he's in..."

"Gallio? You've seen Herod recently?"

Gallio took a deep breath. It was true; he had recently been at Herod's court and seen Herod at first hand, though he hadn't actually talked to him. But seeing him distantly and exchanging words with his courtiers was enough.

"Yes, I've seen him. Only last month. And I must tell you, my brothers, unpredictable he certainly is. But it's much worse than that. The king is ill, very ill. The doctors despair, they have tried all they can, but either he doesn't care or the sickness is beyond them."

"I first saw him forty years ago," said Yazdegerd. "In those days he was young and handsome, slim and fit. People followed him not just because he was king but because he was such an evident leader. He just exuded power and confidence. You knew that if you were with him, you would win, whether it was a fight or an argument. He was engaged then in the campaign that changed his life, capturing and slaying the Galilean bandits - the actions that made Caesar Augustus appoint him King of Judaea. He was a golden leader then. But not without his critics. You know he acted right outside the law? Killing without trial or judgement? Crucifying even? You know he was nearly put to death until the judges panicked? He's been through some times. I saw him again ten years ago, at the great feast and gift-giving after he finished building the Caesarea Maritima. So how does he look now, Gallio? A little changed, I gather?"

Gallio cast his mind back to the appalling sight he had glimpsed. Of a man hopelessly overburdened with fat with a stench from the body that was so strong that even the war-tough bodyguards could not stay a full watch. He described the man he had caught sight of and added, "I think we should be very wary of Herod. As you say Perozadh, he is not a man in control of himself."

"So what do we do?" demanded Caspar. "Slink round the back of Jerusalem, hoping the court does not notice us passing through, and then on to - to where? We don't know where this king is to be born. We need Herod. We need his help. We need to be on the same side.

And even more importantly, we must convince him we're on the same side."

Melchior joined in. "Caspar is right Gallio. We have to do it properly. We'll be careful, don't worry. But we have everything to gain by going about it the right way. We can achieve something for ourselves both with Herod and the new king."

Melchior's voice had that air of authority about it which they all recognised as the final word on the subject. The oldest and therefore officially the wisest of them all, when Melchior adopted that voice that was what would happen.

For a while the talk was liberally spiced with wine and food, the noise level growing and spirits rising to match. But Basantor was still muttering; he hadn't liked being put down. He took an old friend, Karsudas and a relative newcomer, Lucan, into an antechamber.

"We should think about this, my friends," he said, the effects of the drink receding a little as he marshalled his thoughts.

"But we can't go against Melchior," protested Karsudas. "He's the leader - has been for years. You can't split us into two."

"Why not? There's nothing magic about the number eleven. So what if it's only eight? We three can go our own way. There's nothing to stop us. Just keep away from Jerusalem and the old king. It'd be a great deal safer, and we'll achieve the same thing."

"All right," said Lucan, "suppose we do as you say. We'll be a bit of a small band, travelling that far. We'd be an easy target for bandits. And what do we do when we get there? We've got to ask someone where the new King of the Jews is."

"If he is the new King of the Jews, it won't be surrounded with secrecy," retorted Basantor. "Everyone's going to know. It'll hardly be difficult to find him."

"Sorry," said Karsudas, "but if he is the new King of the Jews, he'll be dead before he's breathed his first hour. They're right, Herod won't give him a chance."

"All right," said Basantor, "all the more reason for not going at all. I vote we give it a miss. It's too much like trouble to be worth it."

"And miss the event of a lifetime? Well, I'm afraid I'm not going to miss it. Sorry Basantor, you're on your own here."

Lucan nodded his agreement. "I'm with Karsudas. All right, so we'll have to be careful, and perhaps we'll manage to persuade Melchior not to go via Herod, but we can't miss this. It's the biggest thing we Magi have predicted for centuries."

Basantor sat down and took another drink. He felt he was right, but he also knew that the Magi of all people should not miss such an event. He would just make sure he was not in the team who confronted Herod.

The following morning a small sub-committee met, comprising Caspar, Jairus, Perozadh and Balthazar. Their task was to decide on the cross-country route from Babylon to Jerusalem.

Jairus, best draughtsman among them, had already laid out a large sheet on which he had marked the most important places. Babylon itself was shown on the right in the east, Jerusalem the destination on the left in the west. The Mediterranean Sea was on the extreme west beyond Jerusalem and just above the Red Sea. On the east was the Caspian Sea to the north and the Persian Gulf to the south. And in between, stretching unwelcomingly between east and west - between where they were and where they were going - was the Arabian Desert.

"Well?" Jairus looked up while the others admired his handiwork.

"How far is it?" asked Caspar.

"As the crow flies? About five hundred and fifty miles."

"And that's straight across the desert."

"It is. And I wouldn't recommend it." This was Balthazar speaking up for the first time. "I've tried that once. And that wasn't even in the summer. I tell you my friends, if you want to get yourself baked to extinction and dehydrated into the bargain, that's the way to go. But you'll go without me."

Caspar laughed. "Don't worry Balthazar, we're not quite as thoughtless as you seem to think we are. Just because you were foolish once doesn't mean we're contemplating doing the same. We'll spend a few more days on the road to get there in one piece. Jairus? What are the real alternatives?"

"Well really there are two. We can't go to the south, because there's nothing but desert there. And we've already got Balthazar's verdict on that! To the north then. Now tell me, can you manage a bit of desert, with a few oases to help matters along? We'll save a hundred and fifty miles if you can."

Caspar looked reflective. "When Ezra and the Israelites returned from exile here five centuries ago, which way did they go?"

"We don't know," said Jairus. "The general belief is the way I was just suggesting. North for a while roughly parallel with the Euphrates to Mari, then cutting through the Syrian desert, stopping at Haleb, Tadmor, Hameth and Kadesh. Then on to Damascus and turning south down beside the Sea of Galilee and the Jordan, along the Pilgrim's Way, the great Mecca route, to Rabbah and then Jerusalem."

"And how far is that?"

"About seven hundred and fifty. Or you can go even further north on from Mari, around what they call 'the fertile crescent' up to Haleh before you turn south. It adds another one hundred and fifty miles but it avoids the desert altogether."

Caspar looked round. Perozadh spoke up: "I vote for the seven fifty route. I can't see us wanting to cook ourselves in the Arabian desert, and neither can I see the necessity for an extra hundred and fifty miles if it's not really necessary. Anyway, if it was good enough for Ezra, it's good enough for me."

"I agree," said Caspar with a note of finality in his voice. "And how long do you think it will take?" He turned back to Balthazar, as the acknowledged most widely travelled of all of them.

"How long is a piece of gut?" replied Balthazar. "It depends how long you want to take. Whether you want to keep up the pace or take it easy, making stops and visits on the way. A fully laden camel, ridden by an expert, can do eighty to a hundred miles in a day. At that rate you could do it in a week or so. If you really wanted to. But I can't see it myself. I can't see the need for that sort of rush. To say nothing of the effects on our poor hindquarters!"

"All right," said Caspar. "Let's be realistic. Say it takes two or three weeks to get ourselves ready: hiring the animals and the men to look after them, getting the stores together and packing them all up, organising all our clothing and so on - and then we set off. Then let's say we go at half the speed you mentioned - forty miles a day. And then allow for stopping at various places for various lengths of times. There'll be a lot of people and places I'll want to see on the way for a start. I say we should allow three months. At least. We're already well into July. So we'd get there at the end of October. If our predictions are right, the birth will be well over by then. The baby should be something like six or seven weeks old; that would be fine. Old enough to know he will survive, but still just an untainted newborn son of God."

"So we start preparations now?"

"We start preparations now," echoed Caspar. "But there is one other thing. We must take gifts. Perozadh - will you look into that? Talk to Tiberius and Lucan, they're always paying homage to someone."

Perozadh grinned; Tiberius and Lucan were well known for taking the opportunity to attend every smallest celebration they could get to.

The next morning the three of them convened; Tiberius even at the early hour of about ten o'clock holding a goblet in his hand. Perozadh wondered if he were ever completely sober.

Tiberius lived up to his reputation by speaking up immediately and loudly. "Gold. What else for a king? Gold, of course. To the new king!" And he raised the goblet cheerfully and downed the remaining liquid. "Aaaagh!" he exhaled loudly and peered round for the skin of wine for a refill.

"Seems right," nodded Lucan, as enthusiastic a celebrator as Tiberius but rather more orthodox in his drinking times.

"The benefit of gold," said Perozadh thoughtfully, "is that we can buy it as we travel. There will be plenty of it on the caravan routes up from Petra to the north. We'll meet them as we go. We'll pay a better price than buying it here where it's had to come so far."

"But..." said Tiberius portentously, having found his supply of wine, "have you considered what form it should take? We can't just hand over gold currency - be a bit unsubtle, don't you think? Might look like we're trying to buy favour."

"We are," said Lucan bluntly.

Perozadh didn't want to hear this. It wasn't entirely true. "Now, now," he said wagging an admonishing finger, "We don't need any of that. But Tiberius is right, we need to choose carefully. What about some gold plate?"

"What about a gold plate?" asked Lucan, conscious he'd overstepped the mark a little and trying to sound constructive.

"Or a crown? That'd be appropriate."

Perozadh thought back to the conversation about Herod. "I can't see the existing king being too thrilled with that idea. The implication's a bit obvious, isn't it?"

Lucan nodded thoughtfully as a new idea struck him. "What about a gold thurible? We can sort of kill two birds with one stone there. The thurible made of gold, and then also give some incense to burn in it."

"That's good," said Perozadh. "Frankincense plays such a fundamental role in Hebrew worship. If we're saying the child's going to be a spiritual leader, not a king like Herod, incense is perfect. Only priests can offer it in worship; it shows we understand. Even Herod might be persuaded the child is not going to be a rival."

"That's done then," said Tiberius happily, "well done, all of us. Gold and frankincense. Excellent choices." And he drained the goblet noisily.

But Lucan's brain was in full flood. "I've thought of something else. While we're on the subject of aromas like incense, what about something a bit more exotic? We've covered the royal and religious aspects, what about something a bit more frivolous? What about something to anoint his clothes? What does the psalm say? - 'all thy garments smell of myrhh'."

"Excellent," said Tiberius, "well done, all of us. Let's tell our esteemed leaders."

They got Melchior, Caspar and Balthazar together and outlined their suggestions.

Lucan looked across at Melchior enquiringly and was surprised by the solemn look on his face. Lucan had thought it was a good idea. But Melchior's response surprised him even further.

"Maybe it's a better idea than you perhaps realise Lucan my friend. You know what else myrhh is used for? Embalming. This new king will one day die, if only to demonstrate he is human too. If he is to be the spiritual leader the prophets say, he is not going to find life easy, from Herod onwards. My belief is that there will be much suffering attached to this new sort of king. I think myrhh is perhaps the most important of all our gifts."

Even Tiberius looked thoughtful at this. He put his goblet down and nodded as sagely as he could, leaning against the table to steady himself. "Gold, frankincense and myrhh," he said. "Well done everybody."

CHAPTER 8

THE JOURNEY

Back in Nazareth a few weeks later there was alarm in the town.

Someone had already seen them, the Roman messengers with their soldier outriders, approaching from the main caravan route, and the news rapidly got around. They were not known for their lightness of touch, these Romans.

The shopkeeping Jews took themselves off the narrow streets, well experienced in the ways of the soldiers, and took as many of the provisions for sale back into their houses as they could. The Romans were not very good at paying.

The thunder of hooves announced their arrival. As ever they rode up quickly, taking little account of any unfortunate chickens or goats that happened to be in the way. They weren't too careful with people on foot either; every town had its maimed citizen who had come into contact with a passing Roman on horseback.

They passed noisily down the street which led to the main square and reined their horses in while the messengers posted up their notices, turned abruptly, and galloped out of the town again, stopping only to pick up some fruit from a stall whose owner hadn't been quick enough. The townsfolk crowded round to read the notices.

Stephanos the shepherd had been ahead of them. It was the announcement of the census, ordered by Emperor Caesar Augustus, implemented by Governor Quirinius, taxing every citizen in the Roman Empire. And causing them to return to the region of their family line, which in Joseph's case meant Bethlehem, seventy miles away. For Joseph and Mary, now eight months pregnant, it was a problem they had never even thought about.

Like all Jews, they hated the very idea of a census. Not only for the fact that it was the forerunner of taxes they would have to pay, but for the much more fundamental reason that it demonstrated once again how the Jews were forced to be subservient to the Romans, when the only entity the Jews really believed they should be subservient to was God himself.

Each and every one of them had to take an oath of obedience to the Emperor. The Jews were a proud race and, despite the many physical benefits which Herod as the instrument of Rome had brought them, they never forgave the Roman Empire for inflicting such degradation upon them.

The tax itself was a serious burden too. Ever since Pompey had taken over Jerusalem sixty years earlier the Jews had had to pay a double tax to the Romans: a variable poll tax based on the level of income of every Jewish man or woman in Judaea, and a second tax calculated on the amount and value of land the family owned.

The purpose of the census was to record the names, ages, professions and fortune of each family in a public register so that the levels of payment could be calculated. And now Joseph had a particular worry: it looked as though the census and the birth might coincide. How would the heavily pregnant - or newly delivered - Mary manage waiting for an hour or probably much more in the heat of late summer to be seen? He also thought she was fairly unlucky in having to go at all. It most cases it was just the head of the family - the father or husband - who had to present himself at his family home village or town. But with Mary's parents being so old and now not working at all, she was classed as an "heiress"; a woman of property and some (though not much) money. She had to go to the census, despite her pregnancy, to see what she too would have to contribute to the taxes.

But even so for Mary there was something of a silver lining to the cloud. Despite the fact that Joseph had married her when he could have despatched her to the synagogue and the stoning, people had soon come to realise that she had been pregnant. Joseph had told no-one of his reasoning for the marriage and while some people had simply believed they had anticipated the moment when they finally shared a dwelling, not at all uncommon when engagement was such a binding contract, there were others who were only too ready to believe the story that was going round that Mary had allowed herself to be seduced by the Roman soldier Panthora.

For this reason alone Mary was grateful to get away for a while. She was not to know it would be more than two years before she returned to Nazareth.

Joseph was strong, older, male - and had none of her personal worries. He knew why he had done what he had done in marrying her and cared little for other people's view. He cared little for what the Roman Empire had done, either. As a village carpenter he was content to stay in Nazareth, surrounded by friends and customers. The great works that the Romans had produced - the vast and ornate palaces, the fabulous marble buildings, the huge and elegant public squares - had little attraction for him. And he would certainly have done without them if he could have been spared the taxes. If the straight well-furbished roads and astonishing viaducts made travel easier he was not particularly ready to acknowledge it. Like all Jews, he would prefer to stay where he was without any Roman interference.

And also like all Jews, he had little time for Caesar Augustus, the first emperor of the Roman Empire. Originally called Octavian, he was the adopted son - actually the great nephew - of Julius Caesar, from whom he had taken his new first name. His second name, Augustus, was awarded to him by public demand. That is to say that the public were told to demand it. It meant "the revered one" and was a tag he thoroughly enjoyed. He had commenced his rule some twenty five years earlier and in this census he was carrying on work that his father had started. Julius Caesar had commissioned the first ever comprehensive survey of the empire and had died while it was still being carried out. It had taken thirty two years in all to complete, and Augustus had been responsible for finishing it. This new census was based on the original, but even so would take some two years to complete.

For Joseph though, travelling to Bethlehem did have one attraction: the chance to see some of his relations again. Bethlehem was the recognised home of the line of David, of which Joseph was a proud member. And if the baby was to be born there, a baby that was a child of God - if not *the* child of God - what more appropriate place could there be than the home of that great line?

The moment for departure arrived very quickly. When Mary had set off to visit her cousin Elizabeth in Hebron nearly nine months earlier she had no idea she would be retracing many of her steps much later in the year. The census had not been announced then and Mary had seen that visit as probably her one and only long journey away from her home in Nazareth.

Travelling was much harder now. The whole of Judaea seemed to be on the move, with perhaps half the heads of households journeying back to the area of their birth or their family home. And it was hot. Although the worst of the summer had passed, there was still unbearable heat from well before mid-day until the early evening meal. Much of the terrain offered no shelter and in the state she was Mary knew the journey was likely to be deeply uncomfortable.

And there was yet another problem. Because there were so many people on the move it was well-nigh impossible to find any transport. Joseph cursed himself for not thinking about this earlier. The little donkey that Mary had borrowed from her friend last time had already been booked and was heading somewhere over towards Haifa.

Joseph would have liked to have hired a donkey and cart to give Mary a more comfortable ride but such luxuries had quickly been snapped up.

For a while he had thought they would both simply have to walk; a hugely demanding task for a pregnant girl, even one as strong and healthy as Mary. The Romans would not be interested in her problems and the couple were bound by an immutable law to present themselves in Bethlehem on the due date whatever their circumstances.

Joseph forced himself to trail the length and breadth of Nazareth begging for a favour. He started with friends, moved on to acquaintances, finally tried his richer customers. At what was going to be almost his last stop, an elderly farmer with a smallholding on the very edge of Nazareth, he found luck - of a sort.

"Yes, there is a donkey I could lend you. But Menci is old, fifteen this year. She is a good friend but I don't know how strong. You'd have to pay me if anything happened to her, you understand? I can't make any guarantees."

Joseph would have accepted anything. Promising to take the greatest care of Menci he led her away back to Mary. The whole journey was so fraught with difficulty that he couldn't think beyond just getting there. If Menci was not strong enough to return, that was just another difficulty to surmount. He hoped and prayed that indeed God would provide.

For Mary this was a repeat performance. Except that in place of the cold and unfriendly landscape of her last journey, the roads were now white and blisteringly hot. For most of the journey it was the same route she had taken to Elizabeth, right down towards Jerusalem, but branching east a few miles earlier instead of south towards Hebron.

The overnight stops were the worst. Once again, with half the country on the move, it was next to impossible to find lodgings. Once they had to stay in the open, tucking themselves up within a thicket of undergrowth, fearful of the jackals they could hear in the distance and uncomfortably short of water as they hadn't managed to find anywhere to refill their skins.

Menci seemed to be doing well. They didn't push the old donkey hard but as Joseph had been told, Menci was a good friend and plodded on stoically with Mary perched on her back and Joseph helping out as best he could by carrying much of their baggage himself.

But it was getting hotter even than usual for the time of year. Mary didn't complain but Joseph was tempted to curse the God that had made life so difficult for them. More than once he wondered whether he had been right to accept Mary's pregnancy and the problems it was bringing when no-one would have blamed him for sending her away.

The sky above them during the day was like an oven-lid; pressing the heat down on them and giving no hint of refreshing breeze. In the olive groves to each side they could hear the continual chirruping of the grasshoppers; a steady rhythm which seemed to march along beside them.

Menci's feet were kicking up a cloud of dust with every step that settled ever more deeply upon the travellers. Quickly each day both were covered in a white mist which somehow made the heat even more oppressive, capturing the unforgiving sunlight and tying it to their bodies.

As they began to approach Bethlehem, from each side of the road the white stone walls reflected the heat towards them. In the chinks of the stone lived the lizards; small brown creatures who came out to the road, then lay still as death except for the tiny throbbing in their throats as they breathed. Then suddenly as Menci neared them they would whip into life and dart at the speed of slithering light back to the safety of the walls.

Up on the hillside there could sometimes be heard the sounds of a shepherd boy amusing himself on a pipe. Occasionally they would meet a shepherd on the way, often carrying a lamb or injured sheep across his shoulders, his face burnt almost black with the sun, plodding stolidly on from one place to another, perhaps to the animal doctor, or to deliver the lamb for sacrifice, or even hand over a gift to a loved one's family.

And all the time there were the other travellers, crossing hither and thither over the roads and tracks, each heading towards his birthplace to register for the hated census. They would exchange glances as they passed, the occasional woman seeing Mary's state and offering a prayer for her and her unborn child, all acknowledging the trial they were suffering at the hands of the unpopular rulers.

And there was another problem - which Mary had forbore to tell Joseph so far, thinking he had enough to worry about. She was beginning to feel that her time was near. She had had one or two minor contractions and was thanking God that they were now on the outskirts of Bethlehem.

As they got to the little town they could see it was seething with life. Joseph, who had hoped that his rarely seen kinsmen would have somewhere for them to stay, began to worry. The main street was lined with shops and workshops; so narrow it was well-nigh impossible for Menci to find a way through. They stopped at the entrance to the street and found a patch of shade for Mary and Menci to wait in while Joseph set off to try to find somewhere for them.

They had already tried the public caravansary outside the town and had found it full to overflowing. Bethlehem was some two miles off the main travel route and so there were no inns in the little town itself. It seemed to Joseph as though the main street and the smaller ones off it were like an ant heap: people scurrying in all directions, seeking somewhere to stay or food if they had been lucky enough to find a resting place. His sense of despair was growing. He tracked down an elderly cousin, Andrew, who looked at him hopelessly and shook his head without speaking. There was no need for speech.

"And there's another thing," Joseph said to Andrew, now beginning to feel desperate. "Mary is with child; I don't think it will be long. We must find somewhere and someone to help. Do you know a midwife you can recommend?"

"At least I can help you there," said Andrew, "Old Salome, she has delivered for our family for generations. I will tell her so she is ready when you need her. But I cannot help with somewhere to stay. As you can see, Bethlehem is bursting."

Joseph thanked him and said he would get in touch again as soon as they needed Salome, at the same time in despair at their plight. He wandered around and felt a failure. He had brought his wife all this way, heavy with child, and had not managed to find a place for them.

He reflected on the irony of the name of the town. Bethlehem. It meant "the house of bread". It was supposed to be a town of plenty; a town rich in food and work, which offered much to its people. But to this traveller, in a time of real need, it could offer nothing.

Joseph was on his way back to Mary, waiting patiently on Menci, to reveal the depth of their problem when he was accosted by a man who, judging by his sunburnt appearance and raglike clothes, was probably a shepherd.

"Here for the census? Looking for somewhere to stay?" asked Stephanos.

"Yes, yes," said Joseph, barely allowing himself to feel even a hint of optimism. "Can you help? I've got a wife; she is with child. We must find somewhere quickly."

"You've found exactly the right person," said Stephanos, already starting to lead Joseph along the street, "where's your wife?"

Joseph pointed forwards. "Straight ahead, waiting at the end in the shade there. With the donkey."

As they approached, Joseph felt his heart lurch. For Mary was plainly unwell. She was still sitting on Menci, but her body was drooping and her eyes closed. Joseph couldn't tell whether she was simply tired, overheated and perhaps dehydrated in the oppressive humidity or whether the birth was a stage nearer. From the way that she was sitting, crouched forwards, her hand resting on her stomach, he suspected the latter. He gave thanks for Stephanos and his promise of help but prayed at the same time that this lowly shepherd could really provide the shelter they needed.

But the shepherd seemed purposeful. Immediately taking up Menci's rein and grasping one of their bags in his other hand, he led the way out of the town.

Mary had jerked awake at the sudden movement but looked too unwell to ask anything.

Joseph took her hand and gave her an encouraging, if anxious, smile. "It's all right," he whispered. "He's going to take us somewhere to stay."

Even in her distressed state, Mary found enough spirit to smile back, even if the smile plainly questioned whether such a ramshackle heap as Stephanos could really be trusted to do anything useful.

But Stephanos continued purposefully for two hundred yards before he stopped before what looked like little more than a cave by the side of the road.

"My friend Ephraim's house," he said by way of explanation. "Come in."

With unexpected gentleness he helped Mary down from Menci and led her carefully inside, ducking low in the doorway, leaving Joseph to tie the donkey up and follow inside with the bags.

It was dark inside and at first sight Mary could see very little. But at the back there was a tiny aperture in the rock, through which a little light was emerging and which began to make the room visible to her.

From the gloom, a man appeared.

"You are welcome to my home," said Ephraim, who looked in not much better shape than the shepherd. "We will all have to share it, but you will be safe from the weather and the bandits."

Joseph had by now come in and was greeted by Ephraim. Once his eyes grew accustomed to the darkness he looked around at their resting place.

The house appeared to consist of two rooms only, separated by a small flight of perhaps eight or nine steps. Ephraim clearly lived in the tiny upper room, for though it was almost completely bare of furniture, Joseph could see a rolled up piece of matting and some blankets, which appeared to be Ephraim's bed. In the corner of the room was a rough hewn table, on which was a sieve and some grain; Ephraim had apparently been attempting some kind of meal preparation. There was one small broken-down chair. In another corner were a few vessels and apart from a tiny wooden stool, very little else.

Joseph turned his attention to the room below. There were several clues as to how it was used. The floor was thinly covered with straw which had plainly seen better days. Carved out from the side of the rock wall was a low trough. And fixed next to the trough some iron rings with various ropes trailing beneath them. Joseph looked up at Ephraim.

"Two sheep, two goats and chickens," Ephraim answered. "I'll bring them in later. It'll be a bit of a squash, but we'll manage."

Joseph nodded silently and looked across at Mary. In return she gestured with her head towards Stephanos and Ephraim. Joseph looked back, to see the pair of them standing with their hands held out.

He was just beginning to ferret around in one of the bags for some money when the silence of the house was shattered by a piercing cry.

CHAPTER 9

THE HOUSE OF BREAD

The cry was from Mary and was precisely what Joseph didn't want to hear at that moment. *Please, lord, let us settle into our home first.* But it was not to be.

After that first cry, the pain of contraction taking Mary by surprise, she remained quiet but simply nodded at Joseph. Following his first moment of shock he turned to Stephanos and asked if he knew Salome, the midwife.

Stephanos, who it transpired seemed to know everyone, said the brief word "Yes" and sped out of the house to find her.

Ephraim at first looked as though he regretted allowing Mary and Joseph into his house but quickly pulled himself together and asked what he could do to help.

Joseph, the experience of two other children behind him, knew there were probably many hours to go yet, but said they would eventually need water, warm if possible, and somewhere to lay the baby. And if Ephraim could keep the animals out for the time being...?

Glad to have something to do, Ephraim shooed the smaller animals outside and tied up Menci to a nearby hook in the wall. Then he started to gather up his few skins and go to houses nearby for more and then fill them all with water. He collected kindling and sticks and laid a fire outside to heat the water when the time should come, and then sat down to ponder how on earth you made a bed for a baby. It was not an experience he had had before and could not decide whether to be excited or terrified.

The contractions were some time apart as yet and Joseph simply sat with his wife, talking and comforting her when necessary. It wasn't long before Stephanos arrived back with Salome, a woman of many years. Joseph couldn't make up his mind whether to worry about her extreme age or be comforted by the accumulation of experience she must have had.

But she was more businesslike than she looked and he quickly decided they were in good hands.

Before long Joseph was aware of sounds outside. Looking through the open door he saw people arriving; people he began to recognise as kinsmen he hadn't seen for many years. Clearly Andrew had spread the word through the present line of the House of David and, as was the custom, they were appearing to support Mary through the birth. The few men camped outside; the rather larger body of women all came in, sat around, held Mary's hands in turn, encouraged her and tried their best to divert her when the pain was strong.

They all knew the danger. As many as half the number of new mothers could die in childbirth. There was little anyone could do to take the pain away and if anything went wrong, little they could do to recover the situation. And the circumstances of the birth were not exactly free from the danger of infection: to deliver a baby in the same room as animals, animal dung and straw was asking for trouble. But there was little alternative.

Mary was lucky. The labour was not overwhelmingly long, Salome was calming and efficient, the baby was healthy and cried strongly.

For Joseph the moment he first saw the child was never to be forgotten. The world seemed to go quiet; he could hear nothing of the normal sounds - no birds, no animals, no working in the fields, no man or woman walking or talking. He felt as though he were in a moment frozen in time; even the light seemed to go.

And then Salome spoke very slowly and deliberately as she stared at the child she had just delivered.

"Today I have seen a wonderful thing. Today salvation is born to Israel."

Mary was still dazed with the pain and the exertion and the exhilaration of having given birth. Despite this, in her heightened mood the extraordinary words made Mary think back to her dream. How could Salome have said such a thing if the words of the man had not been true? Yet even at this moment, when Mary like any woman who had been a mother for only a matter of minutes was feeling that unique mixture of relief and euphoria, she could not bring herself to believe she had borne the Messiah. A child of God, yes. But *the* child of God? A new pure life that might affect many in the future, possibly. A man who could one day help lead his race against the oppressors, yes, perhaps even that. But the Messiah?

Then unexpectedly Ephraim spoke up. "The prophet Micah. Did he not say 'Thou Bethlehem Ephratah, though thou be little among the thousands of Judah, yet out of thee shall He come forth unto me that is to be the ruler of Israel'?" Mary knew the quotation well, as she knew all the scriptures. But it only served to make her more confused.

She was not alone though. Everyone was silent, trying to absorb what Salome and Ephraim had said. It was true that the Jews had long expected their saviour to come and lead them. And what Ephraim had remembered so precisely were words that were etched into the minds of everyone who lived in Bethlehem and well beyond. And wasn't Joseph of the line of David? From whom every Jew expected their saviour one day to be born?

Could it be true?

The silence lengthened until it was almost unbearable. And then the new-born child gave his second lusty cry and everything was released. The world started again.

Salome wasted no time in cutting the cord and bathing the child in Ephraim's warmed water. She then produced olive oil to smooth and anoint the skin, and finally salt which she rubbed all over the tiny body to prevent infection.

That done, she handed the child to Mary.

Mary was for a moment nonplussed. But her newfound cousins and aunts were ready for the moment and had brought strips of linen with them, which they handed over to Mary. Cautiously she began the unaccustomed task of wrapping the infant, all arms and legs in the wrong places, in the swaddling clothes; a task she was to repeat every day for the next six months. Swaddling clothes were for more than just warmth: they were tightly bound to restrain the child from its automatic thrashing movements, so that the limbs would grow straight and long.

Just once a day the child would be released from its wrapping; washed, rubbed with olive oil or dusted with powdered dried myrtle leaves, and then securely swaddled again.

Mary was aware of Ephraim again, materialising at her elbow, smiling awkwardly but proudly and pointing to the low trough carved out of the rock wall. It was, Mary had realised by now, where the animals ate from. But Ephraim had cleared and cleaned it and filled it with fresh straw. It was the new child's resting place.

"And what are we to call your son?" enquired Salome, sitting on the floor to rest now that her exertions with the birth were over.

Mary had no hesitation. She remembered the words from the dream, and fortified by Salome's own words said the name immediately.

"He is to be called Jesus."

"Jesus?" echoed Salome, who had received more names in her time as a midwife than she could ever remember and was by now an authority. "The Greek name for Yehosua. Of course. For Yehosua means 'Jehovah is salvation'." And then she repeated her own words. "'Today salvation is born to Israel. Of course." And remembering what Mary had said, Joseph added, "As the prophet Isiah says then we should also call him Emmanuel - 'God is with us' ".

Now the men came in, having left what they considered due time for Mary and the women to have recovered from the birth. They crowded around the manger where Mary had by now laid the baby Jesus, and prayed and admired. Joseph did the opposite and went outside. He needed air.

He was almost immediately joined by the shepherd Stephanos, who felt it was time he was off, if only to find some more travellers looking for shelter. But before he left he felt he should say something, so retreated into the time-honoured question: "So what do you think of your new son, Joseph?"

Joseph, shaken and exhausted, and who had stepped outside because he was dazed by the whole event, felt even more dazed by the routine question.

"My new son?" he repeated automatically, "He's the Son of God more like."

If asked he would not have known exactly what he had meant by his answer. Probably he would have claimed it was what any new Jewish father might have said. For wasn't every new child a child of God? But it might have meant a great deal more.

Stephanos looked hard at Joseph. Already puzzled and unnerved by what he had heard and seen inside for a second, he was quite shaken by this latest remark. The Son of God? He turned and ran, his idea of finding more travellers forgotten. He didn't know what to believe. Like Joseph, he needed some air.

Jesus had been born in the afternoon and within an hour all the relations had disappeared, leaving the new family to recover and get used to the idea of a new baby. Even Ephraim had found an excuse to leave his own home.

But three hours later the peace was broken.

In twos and threes the relations returned, bearing ingredients for a feast - an event that was traditionally to be repeated every night for a week.

The men erected a table just inside the doorway - and because it wasn't big enough, an extra bit outside too - constructed from bits of wood they found behind Ephraim's house, and concocted various stools and seats to sit upon.

The women started to busy themselves around the small fire that Ephraim had upstairs in his own room, decided that too was not big enough, and resurrected the larger one outside that he had used to heat the water for the birth.

The food was simple and healthy and varied only slightly throughout the week. They baked pitta bread on the fire, warmed red and green lentil soup, cooked meat and fish. To the hot food they added fresh vegetables: grains, olives, onions, eggs, houmous, lettuce, cucumbers, almonds and goat's cheese. To follow there would be a selection of fruit: grapes, pomegranates, figs, pears from Syria, date paste and honey.

They had even brought vessels to eat from: woven baskets and pottery bowls, many of which were precious and had survived for generations and were only used on such occasions.

The mood was excitable and noisy, more than Mary and Joseph could really cope with. The chickens and goats had wandered in and Menci, now allowed in, was adding his own particular aroma to the celebrations. By the end of the first feast on the first evening the new parents were totally exhausted. Still barely recovered from their journey and all the anxiety that it had brought, and followed by the birth itself, they had yet to face the first night with a new child.

When Stephanos ran away from Ephraim's house he headed straight back to the fields of Beit Sahur. He was shaken by what he had heard and simple man that he was, didn't know what to believe.

Like all Judaeans he had been expecting the Messiah all his life. But there was a difference between a vague ever-present expectation and reality. He was both frightened and baffled. It was surely not possible that he had led the parents of the Messiah to his birthplace.

At first he had intended to burst out with the news but the nearer he got to Misael and the others the more he felt rather sheepish. All he had heard, after all, was Salome speaking rather extravagantly - probably no more than the excitement following a birth - and Joseph saying his son was more likely the Son of God. But any new father might say that.

He began to feel he was over-reacting. And there was another thing. Cyriacus with his religious fervour was too excitable by far; he had already claimed in the past to have seen visions. Any suggestion that the Messiah might have been born would send him into paroxysms of alarm. Stephanos thought he didn't need that.

So by the time he arrived he had decided to keep quiet about the whole episode and contented himself with telling them how successful he had been with his little money-making scheme. Not bad at all, in fact, for Mary and Joseph were the ninth set of people he had found lodgings for that week.

Acheel, cynic though he was, was forced to agree it was all working quite well. And even Misael, who had the task of making sure the flocks were properly guarded whilst Stephanos was away, had to admit it was a good idea.

After a hot day it was a warm evening and it was a long time after nightfall before the shepherds drifted off into sleep. As usual they took it in turns; Cyriacus was staying awake for the first shift while the other three slept, but after his extraordinary day Steph found himself wide awake too. Cyriacus was glad of the company, for the night watches could be long and lonely.

But despite his earlier decision, in the end Stephanos couldn't stop himself telling Cyriacus about the birth. He started by just telling the story of how he had led the very pregnant Mary and her husband Joseph to Ephraim's tiny house. But then inevitably he found himself describing the birth and then before he could stop himself repeated first the words that Salome had used, and then what Joseph had said about his son.

Predictably Cyriacus immediately looked as though he were about to explode and stared wildly back at Stephanos as he unfolded his story. When he had finished, Cyriacus turned enormous eyes up to the heavens and sat in total silence. Stephanos waited for a further reaction, but the wait turned to be so long that he found himself getting sleepy. Having at last got his story out, he finally felt able to rest, lay back and closed his eyes.

It seemed he had only been asleep for seconds before he felt Cyriacus shaking him.

"What?" Stephanos enquired irritably, his rest disturbed when it had barely started.

"Can't you see?" hissed Cyriacus. "The light."

It was certainly lighter than it should have been at that time, but it was not totally unusual.

"So?" said Stephanos, "so it's a bit light. So what?"

"I think something's happening," whispered Cyriacus.

Stephanos sat up and stared around. Nothing was happening that he could see, though Cyriacus was right, it was unusually bright. Stephanos looked at Cyriacus, who now seemed to be in a world of his own, staring upwards and oblivious of Stephanos's enquiring face.

And then Cyriacus started to speak. Very quietly, almost to himself, he said, "Can't you hear? He says we shouldn't be afraid. He has good news, news of great joy, for everyone. Can't you hear Stephanos?"

He was by now holding tightly onto Stephanos's arm, and Stephanos felt himself being drawn into Cyriacus's vision. "I don't know...tell me, what do you see? What are you hearing?"

Cyriacus continued to look upwards and the words when they came were hard to hear. "He says in Bethlehem, in the city of David, our Saviour is born, just as you said Stephanos."

"Go on," said Stephanos, unable to hear or see anything for himself, but caught up in his friend's excitement and willing to believe that Cyriacus could see and hear things that he and others could not. "Go on, what else is he saying?"

Cyriacus turned to him and spoke with an intensity it was impossible not to get drawn into. "He says the Saviour is coming, that he is the Messiah - the Christ in our language. And that the Christ is the Lord."

74

The Lord, as Stephanos well knew, was the word everyone used instead of Jahweh, the name that was too sacred to be spoken aloud. It was the ultimate word for God.

And now Stephanos, intoxicated by the strength of Cyriacus's belief and the excitement that shone from his eyes, felt that he too could understand and stared up into the sky where he would later claim that he saw a vision of angels. He felt that the message was especially for him, for one of the angels said, "You will find the baby wrapped in swaddling clothes, lying in a manger".

"Yes," breathed Stephanos, clutching Cyriacus's arm so strongly it was found afterwards to be coloured raw blue with bruising, "I know..."

Then Stephanos and Cyriacus felt as though they were frozen in time, staring upwards into the unaccustomed light while the angels themselves looked to the heavens and cried, "Glory to God, on earth peace, goodwill to all men". But as they watched, the vision faded and the two shepherds found themselves embracing each other, looks of astonishment on both their faces, feelings of amazing joy in their hearts.

"We must wake the others," said Cyriacus, breaking away and going over to Acheel and Misael to shake them.

In Cyriacus there was no doubt what he had seen and heard. Stephanos was dazed; he thought he had seen a vision of angels, he thought he had been told again where the Messiah lay, he was fairly sure he had participated in something both wonderful and inexplicable.

"What?" said Acheel irritably without opening his eyes. It wasn't done to be disturbed unless there was an emergency.

"Acheel," said Cyriacus, bursting with excitement, "you've got to wake up. The most amazing thing. And Misael, come on. Wake up."

The two shepherds shook themselves awake and sat up, looking dazed and somewhat surprised that it was light.

"What hour is it?" asked Misael.

"It doesn't matter what hour it is - the middle of the night - but something amazing has happened. I can't believe it. You've got to wake up. We've got to go."

"What?" said Acheel again, not any less irritable. "What in the Lord's good name are you talking about?"

"Listen," said Cyriacus, and described what had happened. He was still so excited he could hardly get the words out sensibly and was falling over himself to get through the story as quickly as he could and hurry off to see the newborn Messiah.

Unfortunately for him, Acheel wasn't quite so ready to be overwhelmed.

"For goodness sake Cyriacus, what do you take us for? You've had another one of your visitations, have you? That's fine; just don't expect us to go along with you. Now, if you don't mind, I've got sleep to catch up on, it'll be my watch before I know it."

"Stephanos?" Cyriacus was pleading for help.

Stephanos, still overwhelmed and confused, spoke slowly. "It's true Acheel, something has happened. I definitely saw something. I definitely saw angels. They said it was true. Really."

"Tell them Misael," said Acheel, lying back on the ground, pulling the sheepskin over him and resolutely closing his eyes again. "Tell them we'll talk about it in the morning, if they must."

"Please Misael...." Cyriacus was begging now. "Please, it happened. Stephanos knows. He was there, he told me. Let's go and see the new Messiah. Let's go."

"Stephanos was where?"

"He was there at the birth. Travellers from Nazareth. Tell them Stephanos."

Stephanos quickly told his story: about the birth, about Salome's words, about Joseph's words too.

Misael was torn. Not as cynical as Acheel, he still found it impossible to believe what Cyriacus was saying. But on the other hand... Cyriacus was most persuasive, and it did tie in with what Stephanos had said. He decided on a compromise.

"I'll tell you what. We can't all go, anyway. And we certainly don't need to go now. Think of the father and mother. They'll need all the sleep they can get. Let Cyriacus, Stephanos and me go in the morning and you can stay out of it Acheel. How's that?"

"Fine," said Acheel, turning over and facing away from them all. "So can I get back to sleep now?"

It was early when they went; Cyriacus couldn't rest and wanted no breakfast.

Stephanos led the way back to Ephraim's house.

When they arrived it was very quiet.

"Is this it?" asked Misael. "You're saying the Messiah was really born here? But nothing's happening. The Son of God, born in this little house, with no-one around? You're pulling my leg, Cyriacus, and it's not very funny, getting us out here like this."

If Cyriacus himself was crestfallen at the lack of activity he managed not to show it. "Stephanos - you remember...?" He was pleading again for support and Stephanos nodded.

"Believe, Misael, we're not inventing it. Come on, let's go in."

Tentatively they knocked and entered Epraim's tiny house, bending down to get inside.

"It's very low," muttered Misael.

"As befits a humble birth," said Cyriacus. "Would you expect something grand?"

Misael thought he probably would but felt disinclined to say so. He was trying not to be a spoiler.

Stephanos called out a welcome as they went in and their eyes became accustomed to the gloom.

Joseph, exhausted by the last few days, nevertheless welcomed them as Jews always do to their house.

As they became able to see, the scene that met their eyes was so ordinary that for a moment even Cyriacus felt some sympathy with Misael's point of view.

The child Jesus was asleep in the manger, the straw pushed up around him and the swaddling clothes covering him from top to toe, with just a tiny face showing.

Mary was bending over him, just smoothing the little hair that he had over his shiny head. Joseph was standing beside them, admiring his son and resting one arm around Mary's shoulder as a silent gesture of support.

The animals were still there; several chickens strutting around, the two goats settled down in the corner, Menci standing nearby giving the comic effect of overseeing the whole scene. Ephraim himself was sitting on the stairs, watching with some little pride. No-one was speaking; as Misael had said a minute earlier, nothing was happening at all. Could this really be the birth of the Messiah?

Cyriacus, after his first moment of doubt, was suddenly and gloriously sure. His faith had come to his aid; the expectation of the

Jews for so long was, he was convinced, now satisfied. God had spoken to him in the night, Stephanos had had the good fortune to be there at the beginning and know where it all had taken place, and he Cyriacus still had the bruising on his arm to remind him how Stephanos too had experienced something during that magical moment in the night.

Cyriacus waited no longer but knelt down before the manger, praying silently to himself.

After a moment, Stephanos followed suit, and then even Misael felt the need to go down on his knees, thought he was not exactly certain why.

They stayed there for no more than a minute, then Cyriacus stood up and, embracing both Mary and Joseph, made the most profound speech of his life.

"Your son fulfils the prophecies. We will tell the world that the Saviour is born. This is truly Bethlehem, the house of bread, the house of plenty, the house from which everlasting succour shall come. The Lord God be with you."

Then the shepherds felt that the family needed their time alone and left quietly. As Cyriacus had said, they were going to tell everyone about the heavenly birth. What they couldn't have imagined at that point was how uninterested people were going to be.

CHAPTER 10

BELIEVING

On the way back to the fields near Beit Sahur all three shepherds were silent with their own thoughts.

Stephanos was in great difficulty: his mind was whirling with conflicting ideas. Despite having been involved with Mary and Joseph right from the beginning and being there at the birth, he still had moments when he could not quite bring himself to believe that he had actually seen the Messiah born. Even his belief that he had seen angels in the sky was now a little uncertain. For nothing is normal in the middle of the night; everyone sees and thinks things that seem irrational in the cold light of day. And that little scene in Ephraim's tiny house: surely that was not what was meant by the prophecies of the Saviour coming to defend the Jews against their oppressors? Surely it should have been something grander than that?

Misael was even less sure. Much as it would have been wonderful for this to be the birth of the Messiah, he didn't see how he could believe it. He tried to be objective. What had he actually seen? An ordinary family with a new baby asleep in some hay. With just one onlooker, and that was the owner of the house, if you could call it a house. When it came down to it, that was all.

He was sorry for Cyriacus though. Misael stole a look at him. He was walking a little to one side, a faint smile on his face and looking as though he were mumbling something to himself: prayers presumably.

But Misael need not have been sorry. For Cyriacus was suffering none of the doubts that were assailing the others. He was never to be dissuaded from the belief that the Son of God had been born and that he had been almost the first to be there to welcome him. Perhaps the event itself was not quite as spectacular as he might have anticipated but that was hardly the point. Everything had happened as it should. He - and Stephanos - had been visited by angels and told the news directly. Stephanos had led the holy parents to the house of the birth and even been present. He had even heard Jesus's father say in so many words that his son was truly the Son of God.

Cyriacus had no doubts, but he saw that the others had.

He walked alongside Stephanos and laid an arm around his shoulders.

"Stephanos. You know, don't you, that you have seen the Son of God? You saw the angels in the night, giving you the news. You know that you, of all people, have been blessed by being present at the birth? You must never forget my friend that you have been chosen to be part of the greatest event ever in the history of the Jews."

As the words left his lips he regretted them. Even he, convinced as he was, could see it was asking a lot to regard this morning's visit as so momentous. And from the silence that greeted his words he knew that Stephanos felt the same. In his desire to convince he had had the opposite effect.

He turned to Misael. "What do you think, Misael?"

Misael was still in great difficulty and couldn't answer. He debated with himself while Cyriacus watched him and read his mind. In the end Misael said simply, "You're asking too much".

Cyriacus felt a physical hurt in his stomach. A pain of disappointment throbbed through him. Was all this nothing but a dream? Was he deluding himself just because he wanted to be deluded? Would he have to go back to being just a shepherd with nothing to look forward to but the next meal?

He trudged on, staring at the ground. In deference, knowing his anguish, the others kept silent.

He found himself praying. And found his prayer answered.

He knew what he had seen and what he had experienced. He knew he had seen the Son of God. And he knew it was his duty to make sure everyone else knew as well.

He took a deep breath and set about rallying the troops: "Misael, Stephanos, I know as sure as I am walking this road that we have seen the Messiah. I know that last night I - and Stephanos too, don't forget - was visited by holy angels to tell me. Why else would I have gone to the little house? Why else would I have dragged you there too? Why would Joseph the father have said what he said if it wasn't true? My brothers, we have seen the Son of God! We have seen the perfection and the beauty and the innocence of the truly pure."

If Cyriacus seemed unaware of the extravagance of his language it was not lost on the others. They had never heard him speak like this nor, looking on his face, had they seen an expression like that. Stephanos, who was still only half way there - but couldn't bear to upset Cyriacus - gave in. For the time being, at least.

"You are right Cyriacus, I believe like you do." He turned to Misael and put an arm around his shoulders. "Misael, it's true. What Cyriacus said, it's true, I know it."

Misael found himself wanting to believe. He looked across at his two comrades and saw the light in their faces. Despite his natural caution it was hard to resist. A little uncertainly, he nodded. But it was all that was needed.

Cyriacus whooped with delight. Stephanos's face was suffused with smiles. Despite himself, Misael found himself smiling broadly too.

The three of them marched on back to the fields of Beit Sahur, their arms around each other, the task before them nothing less than persuading the world that the Christ had been born.

For Mary and Joseph it was no easier. The problem was just the same as that which faced the shepherds, especially Misael. They wanted to believe; they wanted desperately to believe. But they had just had a baby, and nothing is normal after a birth, particularly when it is the first of the marriage. Just as Misael had said, it was so much to ask. And then they had to decide what to say to the rest of the family: they had to tell them something. But they knew what a risk it was. Some of the family would believe, some wouldn't. Probably most wouldn't and they would be the ones with the loudest voices. Neither Mary nor Joseph wanted to make themselves look foolish, but already people knew. The shepherds had been there and apparently had had their vision in the night. Salome had said her memorable words, "Today salvation is born to Israel". Ephraim had heard it all.

The more they thought about it, the less it seemed Mary and Joseph could keep the idea to themselves.

The shepherds were already discovering the problem at first hand.

Acheel had stayed consistent and wanted nothing to do with the idea.

Misael had allowed himself to be drawn into Cyriacus's and

Stephanos's excitement - Stephanos now having seemingly fully committed himself.

But when they began to tell others they were not prepared for the responses. Even Misael, who had been sceptical himself, was hurt and surprised when others were sceptical too.

"Jonathan, my friend," said Cyriacus expansively, meeting a cousin at the well, "we have fantastic news...."

But Jonathan had only listened politely, nodded, given Cyriacus a searching look and gone on his way, leaving Cyricaus staring after him in dismay.

"Benjamin!" cried Stephanos, "the Christ is born! We have seen him and prayed with him!"

"Indeed," said Benjamin the seventy-year old, peering up at Stephanos from the ground where he was resting. "And how do we know this?"

Stephanos told the story, realising as he did so that Ben was watching and listening with a degree of cynicism that he had not expected.

"Hannah," started Misael to his wife when he saw her the next day, "you will not believe..."

"No I won't," said Hannah, her arms buried in the stream as she hung over it washing the children's clothes.

Only two people they met had shown any real interest, and even then it was interest tempered with doubt. And the more they thought about it, the more the shepherds could not blame them. For as Misael himself had said, they were simply asking too much. Unless they had been there for themselves, and experienced it all for themselves, how could any Jew really believe that their saviour had come in this way? Without any pomp? Without any proclamation?

And yet, if you asked them how He should come, none of them would have known.

At the evening family feast, the mood was much the same. Most had heard, one way or another, what was supposed to have happened. Many were cynical, some put the story down to the euphoria that accompanies a birth, a few wanted desperately to believe but found it hard.

All found it difficult to accept that the Son of God would be born in this way. At the centre of it all, Mary retreated into herself and pondered.

Four days later the new parents attended the census ceremony.

It was ignominious for the Jews. They were forced to stand in line in the scorching heat while the Roman soldiers and officials took their time. The heat bore down on them relentlessly. The officials slowly made their way along the line of the many inhabitants of the town, none of whom were allowed to leave until everyone was listed. Then each had to swear undying and everlasting allegiance to the Emperor Caesar Augustus; the Jews found it hard to utter the words. And Mary, still not strong after the birth, was beginning to feel sick and Joseph put an arm around her, only to have it removed by a passing Roman officer. Summoning all the strength she could find, Mary managed to last out until they were all unceremoniously dismissed. She bore the experience without comment; she had read enough to know it was always like that and decided the best thing was to try to ignore the treatment they received and give thanks when it was all over and they could start thinking of returning to Nazareth.

But before that could happen two other things had to take place.

The first of these was Brit Milah, the covenant of circumcision, confirming the child as a member of the Jewish people.

The ceremony took place in Ephraim's little house, and because Mary had to be kept apart they used Ephraim's own room, up the steps from where Mary and Joseph were living. The baby was first held and passed around by Joseph's relations before he was handed to the Mohel, the surgeon specially trained for this ritual operation. Immediately before the operation itself, the Mohel placed the little boy on the one and only chair Ephraim had in his house: for the purposes of the ceremony this was the Chair of Elijah and symbolised hopes of redemption. Then the Mohel passed the child to Cyriacus, who to his eternal delight and amazement had been appointed godfather by Mary and Joseph, to hold during the operation.

When this was over, to the accompaniment of lusty cries, the name was announced. He was formally called "Yehosua, son of David", which was immediately and for ever after shortened to "Yesu" or "Jesus".

Then the whole room said together, "Just as Yehosua has entered the covenant, so may he enter the study of the Torah, the wedding canopy, good deeds". After this reference to the traditional history of the world from the Creation to the death of Moses and the extremely brief outline of the life cycle, the ceremony was over and all were ready to celebrate.

The second thing that had to happen before the new little family could return to Nazareth was Mary's purification. She was still considered unclean by Hebrew rules but it was another thirty-two days before this could take place.

Meanwhile the Magi had arrived at Kadesh on the Orontes river, site of two ancient battles, about two thirds of their journey completed.

The party was not quite so jolly as it had been before they had set off. Four hundred miles had taken toll of the strength of the older members of the group; in particular Melchoir, on the verge of being seventy, was looking somewhat worn. But their spirits were good; bolstered by the wine of the evening and ensconced within a large villa owned by a friend of Alphaeus, they were in talkative mood.

"Of course," said Alphaeus, revelling in his position as the fount of local information, "Thutmose the Third has a lot to answer for".

This produced, as he knew it would, looks of bewilderment from his colleagues. Some nodded as though upon thinking about it they knew exactly what he meant. Others continued to look mystified. One, Tiberius, fortified as ever by the wine goblet, spoke back loudly but with a smile on his face.

"Absolutely right Alphaeus."

Alphaeus stared back at him, unable to work out whether he was serious or not. If Tiberius actually did know what he was talking about, Alphaeus was in danger of losing his opportunity to lecture. He tried again.

"I'm talking about this spot, you know. Where we are staying - here at Kadesh. Heaven knows how it would all have turned out if the Prince of Kadesh had defeated Thutmose. At Megiddo, I mean."

"Absolutely," said Tiberius, trying to stifle a smile.

Alphaeus tried yet again. "I take it you all know what this is all about?"

"What do you think?" asked Lucan, playing the game with his old drinking companion.

Alphaeus looked around. The looks of bewilderment on the

others' faces had been replaced by grins. They all knew Alphaeus liked to get on his soap box and it would do no harm to take him down a peg or two.

"I think... I think you've got no idea what I'm talking about." He looked wounded. "All I'm doing is telling you a little about the history of this place. Of course if you don't want to know..."

He turned away in mock indignation. He knew he was having his leg pulled. It wasn't the first time they had taken him on and it was all a bit of a game.

"OK Alphaeus," said Jairus, "tell."

"Ah, well, right," said Alphaeus, quickly taking his opportunity. "It was about fourteen hundred and fifty years ago. The Syrians under the Prince of Kadesh were fighting the Egyptians under Thutmose at Megiddo in Palestine. The Prince lost and Kadesh remained under Egyptian rule for another hundred years or so."

This riveting news was greeted with some degree of silence. Alphaeus felt himself impelled to offer something else.

"And then later Kadesh was captued by Seti the first. And then a hundred years later still the town was invaded by the Sea Peoples."

"And what happened then?" asked Hormizdah with a high degree of mock eagerness.

At this point Alphaeus recognised defeat, refilled his goblet and retired to the edge of the room. Some of the others however were getting into the mood for discussion, and Basantor again brought up the subject of Herod.

"Have you had any more thoughts about Herod, once we get to Jerusalem, Melchior?"

"My thoughts are the same," said the leader, "I don't see what else we can do but approach him. And let's not forget, he's a great man, with great achievements."

"He's a murderer," said Hormizdah uncompromisingly. "He murdered that beautiful wife Mariamne the Hazmonean, whom he only married to ingratiate himself with the Jewish leaders."

"Yes," interrupted Gallio who, as the only one among them who knew Herod at all, felt a little sympathy for him. "But he did really love her. All right, I admit he married her for political purposes, but he did love her too."

"Oh yes?" asked Hormizdah. "And then what happens? He lets his sister Salome poison his mind against her. Salome knows what a jealous and insecure man Herod was and takes the first opportunity she can to cause a rift between him and his wife. And he's so unstable he falls for it, kills Marianme, her two sons, her brother, her grandfather and her mother. And as if that weren't enough, he then disinherits and kills his own eldest son Antipater. He'll go for anyone he thinks is standing in his way and he's only got one way of dealing with them. Do you know what Emperor Caesar Augustus said? 'It's better to be Herod's pig than his son.' I think we'd be playing with fire if we told him what we're doing."

"I must say," said Kaeso, "Hormizdah's making sense. Surely you can imagine how he'll react if he hears we're looking for the King of the Jews. Isn't that what he is supposed to be himself?"

Melchior could see that many of the others were nodding. He gave in. "We've had this conversation before," he said wearily, "and I know what you mean. Perhaps you're right. Perhaps we'd better just see how it goes and see if we can manage to bypass him. Though I don't think it'll be easy. He has his spies all over the place."

Bazantor and Hormizdah silently toasted each other. The old man had seen sense. But he had also seen what they were doing.

"All right you two," he said, "but I'm making no promises. I think it extremely unlikely we'll get out of Jerusalem without Herod knowing. I just said we'd try."

The two youngest of the Magi, Levi and Karsudas, emboldened by the wine which had been flowing freely for the last hour or two, climbed to their feet and pantomimed their way around the terrace, putting one foot silently and stagily in front of the other, mimicking the group trying to avoid Herod's spies.

Amid the laughter this caused, Gallio stayed silent. "I still think you're being a little unfair," he said at last. "He's a great man. I don't think we should overlook that. Judaea owes him a lot. Just think how warlike it used to be there. If nothing else he's brought thirty years of peace."

Hormizdah was more cynical. "He's had a charmed life, I'll give you that. Do you know his biggest stroke of luck? Remember when Octavian - as Caesar Augustus was called then - and Mark Anthony were fighting each other to succeed Julius Caesar after they murdered him? Herod got that completely wrong, supporting Anthony all the way - and that despite the fact that the harlot Cleopatra had used her influence with Anthony to grab a lot of Herod's land. And when Octavian finally wins at Actium Herod owns up to supporting Anthony and still gets made ruler of Palestine. Biggest piece of good fortune I ever heard of. He even got his land back from Cleopatra."

"Ah Cleopatra," sighed Tor, "now there's a woman."

"Woman?" expostulated Perozadh, "she was a monster. Do you know what she did? She was the most ambitious, the most ruthless woman in history. Married her own younger brother Ptolemy and then had him killed so they did not have to share Egypt between them. Then she married another brother and he went mysteriously missing. The Romans hated her."

"What do you expect?" put in Yazdegerd. "She was a woman. Romans don't like powerful women. Especially when they set their sights on their leaders. First Julius Caesar then Mark Antony. She emasculated Antony. He was supposed to be going into battle to win Parthia but she made him soft and he decided he'd rather lounge around her court, feeding her milk and honey. And the rest! No wonder Octavian beat him at sea outside Alexandria. And what did Cleopatra do next? Tricked Anthony into thinking she was dead so that he would kill himself. Which he did, of course. Though she hadn't realised Octavian was going to come after her."

"Well I've got no sympathy for her," said Caspar. "As if being ruler of Egypt wasn't enough. She wanted to take over the whole of the Roman empire. She would have too if Antony hadn't lost out to Octavian."

"Well, you've got to admit she had her head screwed on," said Tor. "When Antony wanted to win Parthia she knew he didn't have enough money or men or food supplies. By offering to help out she got him so much into her debt he even married her - despite already having a wife Fulvia back in Rome."

"Yes, well, when it all settled down, Herod came out of it very well," said Gallio.

"Octavian knew a good leader when he saw one," said Melchior. "He already knew Herod; he knew he had the guts and the political ability to rule Palestine as he wanted. Herod wasn't lucky, Hormizdah, he deserved that position. And knowing his nose for trouble, that's why it's my belief we should be on side with him, not trying to avoid him." But before Bazantor could argue again, Melchior added, "But I've said what I've said. We'll try to keep him out of it."

Melchior's first instincts were right. But unfortunately the Magi were just a collection of priests who were steeped in astrology and not very good at politics. And if the majority wanted something, the majority had the right to it, however badly it might turn out in the end.

CHAPTER 11

THE TEMPLE

Four weeks later Jesus left his birthplace for the first time.

He and his parents were making the five mile journey to Jerusalem. Perched above the ever-striving little Menci and in the lap of his mother, Jesus travelled north to Herod's temple, the place which would become life and death to him. Forty days after the birth, Mary was travelling for the rites of purification and sacrifice. Had Jesus been a girl, she would have had to wait twice as long.

As her first child, according to tradition that went back to the time of the Exodus when Moses led the Hebrews out of Egypt into Sinai, Jesus had formally to be presented to God in memory of him sparing the firstborn of the Israelites who had killed the firstborn of the Egyptians.

The road was busy, just as it had been on the way to Bethlehem nearly six weeks ago. The journey, slow because of the number of travellers still on the road and with Menci unable to be hurried with his burden of mother and child, took nearly two hours. When they arrived at the bustling city Joseph made it his first duty to find a well to refill their skins and make sure Mary had something to drink. It was not as hot as it had been, but very dusty and Menci's small feet and legs were again almost white.

They were bound for the temple, and both Mary and Joseph were nervous. Mary had at first been looking forward to seeing the temple again where she had spent so much of her childhood. But then she had been told that that it was no longer there. King Herod had decided it was nowhere near grand enough for the temple of the capital city of Judaea; he had had the five-hundred year old building knocked down and had constructed a new one in all its enormous glory to ingratiate himself with the Jews.

Yet even the temple that Mary had worshipped at had not been the first on that spot. Almost a thousand years earlier, David's son Solomon had built one there before that, taking nearly seven years to do so. It lasted for about four centuries before the armies of the Babylonian king Nebuchadnezzar destroyed it. Then the Jews, returning to Jerusalem from exile in Babylon, and with the help of the Persian king Cyrus the Great, replaced it with the second - the much more modest structure that Mary knew.

The Jews, and especially the priests, were highly suspicious of the new ruler Herod that the Romans had wished upon them. Herod was leaving not a stone of the previous temple in its place and the priests were convinced that he was going to build some secular monstrosity there that had nothing to do with the sacred purpose of the site.

But they need not have worried; although his motives were not the same as the priests, Herod was certainly going to build a real temple - and it was to be a temple to end all temples.

He hired 10,000 labourers and 1,000 wagons to haul stones for the building. Sensitive to the Jews' fears that the sacred areas might be profaned by the hands of non-believers, he had 1,000 priests trained to be masons and carpenters.

Herod knew all about Solomon's original temple there and was determined to rival, if not beat, it in size and opulence. This was ambition on a grand scale, since Solomon's temple was probably twice the size of the one that Herod was replacing. It even meant Herod had to enlarge the Temple Mount itself - building huge supporting structures into the valleys around it. The temple building took a year and a half to construct; but the whole temple complex, an area of some 30 acres, was not to be finished in his lifetime, nor for many years after.

Mary and Joseph tied Menci up and stood before the broad steps leading up to the huge colonnade that surrounded the temple, the baby in Mary's arms, and felt weak at the knees. The great temple was overwhelming: a huge structure of cream-coloured limestone dressed and decorated with golden gates, many-coloured rich fabrics and marble pillars.

It was a forbidding place for two unworldly village dwellers. Not only for its great size and stateliness but also for the high-pitched noise of a dozen different languages, the restless bustle of merchants and money-changers, the strident sounds of the builders still at work on the vast complex.

Mary and Joseph's first task was the mikveh, the ritual bath in which they had to immerse themselves to ensure their fitness to enter the Temple Mount.

Then Mary was required to make a sacrifice. Had they been richer it would probably have been a sheep, but as a poor carpenter's family it was accepted that they could not afford that. Instead they were going to buy the minimum expectation of two pigeons.

But there was another cost too. It was little enough - only five shekels - but even that would stretch the family purse uncomfortably. The five shekels were part of an ancient ritual. Every firstborn, providing he was perfect in every way and free from any blemishes or defects, was theoretically due to serve the Lord, probably as a priest. But to free him from this obligation he could be "bought back" at the price of five shekels. And since, God-fearing though most Jews were, no-one wanted to commit their sons at so early an age, this small monetary sacrifice freed them from that obligation. The shekels could be handed over to any priest in the Temple.

But first Joseph had to find a money changer. Only Tyrian shekels were acceptable in the Temple, so Joseph had to exchange his own local currency. In the colonnades around the Court of the Gentiles money changers were calling out loudly to attract custom, changing both foreign and local currency into the shekels for the Temple. Amid the din and hubbub, where one day Jesus would find himself arguing with the money changers and lenders, Joseph found one free for a moment and changed his coins, grimacing at the low rate of exchange and the high commission which the merchant demanded.

Passing through the great doors of the colonnades into the Temple Mount the little family found themselves in the huge Court of the Gentiles. Now they were absolutely surrounded by other people, pushing and jostling towards the low stone wall that surrounded the inner courts of the Temple, dealing with the moneychangers, shouting to try to find relatives lost in the throng, bartering with the sellers of animals or birds for sacrifice. They could hardly hear themselves speak, their own words lost in the sea of other languages - Hebrew for the services, Aramaic the language of the street traders, Greek for the scholars and well-to-do, a myriad of other languages and dialects from visitors far and wide.

Joseph bought the pigeons for sacrifice here and felt strange as he walked on, with the two birds clasped in his hand. He was keen to find the place for the sacrifice to take place so that he could put that particular matter behind them.

Pressing on through the crowd and anxious to find a quieter place they climbed a low flight of steps and passed through a gate into the Court of the Women - as far as Mary would be allowed to go.

But there was plenty going on here. Though quieter than the Court of the Gentiles, the smaller area was still thronging with people. More of a socialising place than the outer court, people were talking rather than shouting, praying rather than bartering. To their surprise and relief Joseph spotted one of his cousins from Bethlehem with his family, and the group found an empty spot near one of the chambers in the corners of the Court and gossiped with each other. It was relaxing and reassuring after the huge foreign multitudes they had been passing through to find someone they knew and could talk easily to. The cousin's wife took Jesus from Mary's arms to give her some rest and the two men wandered off a little to meet some of the cousin's friends who were also there. After the aggressive atmosphere of the Court of the Gentiles, this seemed like a refuge.

And it was while the men were away from the women for a few moments that they were approached by an elderly heavily bearded man whom Joseph's cousin introduced as Simeon. Joseph had already noticed him, praying silently in the corner of the Court and had felt there was something especially spiritual and holy about him. He seemed to have an air of patient expectation, as though he had been waiting for something for years and knew for certain that one day his prayers would be answered. Joseph felt he had rarely seen a man more at peace with himself.

"Joseph," said his cousin, "This is Simeon. It would be hard to come here without meeting him - I think this is his second home!"

Simeon smiled; holy he might be but that didn't mean he lacked a sense of humour, and was used to being ribbed by his friends. "One day, my friend, one day..." he said. "And where are you from, Joseph?"

Joseph explained that though from Nazareth, he was currently staying in Bethlehem where he had been for the census and where his wife had borne their child Jesus.

On hearing the names of the child and the birthplace, Simeon looked hard at Joseph. Behind the old man's face his thoughts were racing.

Then he said, "I have been awaiting death these many years, but I am not to die before I have seen Israel's redeemer with my own eyes. The Holy Ghost has told me this in my praying." He continued to stare hard at Joseph, who returned the stare, conscious that without a word from him, Simeon had seemed to sense something.

"May I see the child?" Simeon asked.

"Of course."

They took the old man across to where Jesus was, now back in Mary's arms. Simeon did not reply to the greetings from the women but instead just looked silently at the child. Alarmed, they saw how white Simeon had gone and fell quiet themselves, wondering what was happening.

Without asking, Simeon took Jesus from Mary's arms, who let the child go without demur, somehow knowing he was safe.

Simeon looked down at the tiny boy in his arms and knew his prayers over the years had been answered. The conditions for the birth of the Messiah were fulfilled. It was the greatest day of his life, yet because it was God's will and he was one of God's people he remained calm, gave thanks, and said softly, "Lord, now I your servant can go in peace, as you have said. For now I have seen the salvation you have prepared for us. Light both for the gentiles and your own people of Israel." He handed the child back to Mary, who accepted Jesus without taking her eyes off Simeon. All of them in the group stayed silent, watching the old man as he continued to speak and marvelling at his words.

Simeon, the holy man, blessed them and said to Mary, "Your child is here and ready both for the falling and the rising again of the peoples of Israel. People will speak against him, and it shall be like a sword through your heart. But through this many will find salvation."

He fell on his knees before Jesus and prayed silently, while Mary and the others looked down upon him, finding it hard to absorb what he had said.

And despite being surrounded by hundreds of others - none of whom had any idea what was happening but were used to seeing people like Simeon on their knees in that hallowed place - they all felt that the hand of God was upon them.

Mary and Joseph looked at each other with their eyes speaking for them. The doubts that came and went were certainly gone for the moment. And before the day was out, they would move another step nearer understanding and believing.

With Simeon still on his knees, the sounds of the merchants broke in on their thoughts, reminding them that they had other work to do. The two pigeons were still at Joseph's wrist, flapping noisily. And they still had the five shekels to hand over.

Joseph was confused at first. He could see in the court a number of treasury chests - thirteen in all - shaped like the trumpet of a ram's horn, all open to receive money to help pay for the work of the temple and in particular the costs of all the sacrifices. He was staring at each in turn, trying to decide which was the right one for his purpose, when he was interrupted by his cousin.

"Remember cousin, the money must be handed directly to a priest."

Joseph smiled in gratitude. He realised that had he put the money into one of the chests he would have had to raise another five shekels and do his job correctly. He bowed a blessing to his cousin and found a priest standing and waiting for just such a purpose.

And now the scrabblings of the two pigeons could be ignored no longer. Joseph wondered whether they had inklings of their fate and whether knowledge that they were to be a sacrifice to God in any way lessened their fear.

Taking Mary by the hand, Joseph advanced through the Court of the Women to the Nicanor Gate in the west wall. Together they stood at the foot of the fifteen curved steps looking up in wonderment at the magnificent construction of the gate. Then they turned to look at each other, knowing that Mary was allowed no further, despite the fact it was her sacrifice that had to be made. In fact Mary had had no need to go to the Temple at all if she hadn't wanted to. Silently she handed Jesus over to Joseph and settled the child as best she could in his free arm, the two pigeons still flapping in his other hand.

Then Joseph and his son mounted the steps and entered the third court, the Court of the Israelites, where only Jewish men were allowed. From this narrow strip of stone pavement they got their first glimpse of the high altar, just visible through yet another doorway in the Court of the Priests.

The altar sat alone, made of unfinished stone that metal tools had never been allowed to touch. Each corner was decorated with a carving shaped like a horn.

As they entered this final court they could see behind the altar the most holy inner sanctum, what was really the Temple itself; this was reserved for priests.

It was not quiet there, nor any freer from the bustle that they had experienced in the temple buildings so far. Even so, Joseph felt himself humbled, knowing the tradition that buried beneath the inner sanctum was the sacred rock upon which Abraham, as instructed by God, had prepared to sacrifice his son Isaac.

It was noisy, busy - and smelly.

The smell was overpowering, and came from a unique mixture of incense, charred animal fat and blood from the sacrifices which were going on continually.

Joseph quickly saw that sacrificing was a highly organised business, with a team of priests in charge of the whole process. He watched with eyes wide open as they went about their duties fast and furiously in order to cope with the never-ending flood of people with sacrifices of all sorts. These varied from the small pigeons like Mary's to full-sized bulls according to the purpose of the sacrifice.

Many were for atonement for sins and these would simply be burnt offerings, where the animal's flesh was reduced to ashes on the altar. Others might be peace offerings where only part of the animal were burned; perhaps the kidneys or fat tissue. Peace offerings could be for any number of purposes: a family reunion, a safe return from a journey, a good harvest, a satisfactory deal.

The priests' jobs for the day had been chosen by casting lots. One would be the slaughterer, another would sprinkle blood on the altar, another would clear the ashes, another would keep the ashes burning, another would bring the wood, inspecting as he worked to make sure there were no worm holes and it was as pure as possible.

Nervously, Joseph approached a priest at the altar, showed him the pigeons and explained that the sacrifice was for his wife Mary's purification following the birth of their son. The priest nodded and wasted no time in cutting the throats of the birds and passing them to another priest to splash their blood on the altar. Then the priest placed the animals' remains on the fire and Joseph watched while Mary's sacrifice was consumed by the flames. Before he knew where he was the priests had turned to another applicant and Mary's purification was complete.

Sickened both by the smells and the blood, Joseph hurried back to the Court of the Women to rejoin his wife and tell her the good news that she was now pure again in the sight of God.

But when he got there he found her in conversation with several women he didn't recognise.

Three of them were Mary's own age, but the fourth was far older; in her mid-eighties so far as Joseph could guess.

About to speak to Mary and tell her the news of her purification, something in her face stopped him and he found himself listening with all of them to the old woman.

"Who is this?" Joseph whispered to his cousin, also standing nearby.

"Anna, the prophetess," replied the cousin, "the daughter of Phanuel from the tribe of Aser. A widow, married for only seven years before her husband died. Now she virtually lives in the temple, fasting and praying here night and day."

"What is she praying for?" asked Joseph.

But he got no answer from his cousin, nor needed it after a moment, for they all could hear Anna speaking out, loudly and clearly, to anyone who would listen. She was, in fact, publicly praying.

"Oh Lord on high, we give thanks for this thy child delivered to us. For our saviour, our Messiah, our new lord. We give thanks for the purity of the new-born infant, who is here to help us redeem our sins and ourselves. We give thanks for the end of the years of waiting. And I give thanks that I have lived to see this day, when the Jews for evermore shall be saved."

Joseph could see that Mary was staring transfixed at Anna, and that many of the crowd, which was growing in size by every minute, were doing the same. As Anna stopped for a moment, those in the crowd were turning to each other, whispering and pointing towards Mary and her son Jesus in her arms.

Slowly, Mary separated herself from the crowd, as they stood still surrounding and listening to the old prophetess. She crossed over to Joseph and put her arm out to him, cradling Jesus in her other arm.

"You hear what she says? And what Simeon said? And what the shepherds said? Is it true, Joseph, can it really be true? Is this truly the Son of God here in my arms, born of us?"

Joseph looked back at his wife, remembering the way he had discovered his wife was with child but never understanding how.

And then he looked at the child and recalled his own words to the shepherds, "My son? The Son of God, more like".

And just a glimmer of belief began to stir in his soul.

CHAPTER 12

HEROD

However much the Magi may have debated whether or not to approach Herod, in the end the decision was taken from their hands. As Melchior had said, Herod had his spies all over the place.

Herod had two palaces in Jerusalem: the smaller one in the city itself; the other, which Esther had pointed out to Mary on her journey to Hebron, was Herodium, some twelve kilometres south on a hill rising 758 metres above sea level and with a breathtaking view. To the east stretched the Judean desert and the mountains of Moab, and to the west the Judean hills.

Herod had built Herodium on the site of a famous victory. It was both a fortress and a palace, and where he spent nearly all of his time now as illness and age was overtaking him.

When the Magi were just one day away from Jerusalem, Herod was lying, as he had for so many days now, half strapped, half squashed, into an enormous chair bed. Years ago he had inspired both devotion and fear among his followers in battle and in politics. But he had not taken care of himself. He had drunk too much and eaten too much and taken too many wives. He had also taken too many other women, and had not enquired too much of their background. Today he was reaping the harvest he had sown.

Now his servants, guards and courtiers stayed away as much as they could. Not just from his fearsome temper (never much restrained, now bursting through the surface at the slightest provocation), but quite simply for the smell.

The stench that rose from his body was so overpowering that the servants had taken their lives in their hands and worn linen masks just to be able to breathe. They had feared as they had first put them on that he should have them beheaded for daring to take such action but they had decided it was worth the risk. Better to be dead than to inhale the fumes from the royal body.

Today was a bad day. Herod had not even asked to be raised from his seat to look from the window. He had remained for several hours staring straight ahead at the walls before him, not even turning his head towards the battlements which stretched away from the palace quarters towards the hills. But the peace was suddenly to be rudely broken by a mighty roar from the king.

"Aristobolus!"

The servants, huddled outside the royal door, shuddered. Aristobolus, Herod's most trusted aide and friend, had a temper almost as great as his master. If Herod caused Aristobolus trouble, it was certain they would all be in trouble themselves before the day was out.

Alas, Aristobolus wasn't there.

The servants argued with themselves; Tancred lost.

As he entered the room and approached, Tancred pretended to scratch his nose; in reality he was attempting to deflect the smell from his nostrils.

"Your majesty, I am sorry to inform you that the master Aristobolus is not here. Shall we send to find him?"

Herod's great head slowly lolled sideways to regard the unfortunate servant. Tancred visibly shrank and scratched his nose again. It was hardly his fault that Aristobolus was not there, but Herod was apt to kill people when he was displeased. He had, after all, already disposed of his wife, her two sons, her brother, her grandfather and her mother.

Herod screwed up his eyes, making them almost invisible within the massive folds of his face. "Who is this? Is this the worm Tancred?"

"Yes, majesty."

"Tancred." Herod brooded. Should he have him consigned to the fields to work his fingers off helping bring in the crops or should he have him beheaded? Later. He really wanted Aristobolus. "Go on. Find him. I want him here quickly. Do you understand? Not later today. Not in half an hour. Very quickly."

"Your majesty." Tancred retired as quickly as he dared, scratching his nose again. He nearly made it to the door.

"Tancred!" The royal voice boomed out so loudly that Tancred nearly fell over. "Come here. What is wrong with your nose? Do you want me to pull it off for you? Is that it? Is it troubling you? Bring it here."

Tancred took a deep breath and advanced to his master.

"Here!"

Tancred had optimistically stopped a metre or so away from Herod. "Here!"

The wretched servant stood as close to Herod as he could, his senses engulfed by the smell of sweat and rot that belched from the king. It was all he could do not to vomit.

Herod lifted himself an inch or so from his chair and stared at Tancred's nose from a distance of three inches. Tancred closed his eyes and tried not to breathe. A flabby, putrid hand touched his nose, pushing it back and forth.

"I see nothing wrong with this nose," pronounced Herod. "But we will have it removed if you like?"

In order to reply to his master's sarcasm Tancred had to open his mouth and breathe. "No Sire," he whispered, "it was nothing but a slight irritation." He closed his mouth and stared at Herod, a dangerous act in itself, specially when the king was only inches away.

But Herod was tired and had had enough of the game.

"Go. Find Aristobolus. Find him quickly."

Tancred withdrew, just managing to restrain his exit to a fast walk. Outside the door he fell against the wall, gasping for breath. "You owe me," he said to the others. "Find Aristobolus for God's sake and find him quickly or we'll all be dead."

Ten minutes later Aristobolus entered quietly. The king was asleep and the courtier stared at his master with distaste. They had been friends and allies for ten years now and no-one was closer to Herod. But even Aristobolus himself was finding it difficult these days.

The very sight of his old friend and master appalled him.

Herod's hair had gone and so had most of his teeth. His body, gross and sprawling, was largely covered in swathes of bandages, but thick as they were, they weren't adequate to contain the sores of the skin, which seeped through. On one leg, swollen to twice the size of the other, small white worms could be seen crawling among the folds of bandage.

But the worst was the stomach. Sagging and enormous, it was home to the greatest of Herod's disabilities. No longer able to do its work this it was that gave off the stench. No-one could stay in the room for long and even just beyond the door the servants took it in very short turns to be on watch.

Aristobolus wondered whether he dared leave again and was balancing up the risk when Herod suddenly jerked awake and glared at him.

"Where've you been? I wanted you."

"I – "

"It doesn't matter Aristo. I've heard rumours."

Herod was the only one who called him by the shortened name, and that was only because it was the same as one of his sons and he wanted to distinguish them. Aristobolus wondered what rumours he had heard. He also wondered how he had heard them; most of what Herod gleaned these days came through Aristobolus himself and he was able to filter out any information that was likely to inflame his master. But Herod had not lost all his wiles and not infrequently took Aristobolus by surprise.

"What particular rumours, my wise master?" He was not above trying a slight touch of humour with Herod; both knew the expression was used lightheartedly but both also knew that Herod liked the words themselves.

"The rumour about the new king."

Aristobolus swore beneath his breath. This was one thing he had really wanted to keep from Herod. How on earth had he heard about this?

"It's nothing my lord. Some hysterical yatterings among the peasants who are believing what they want to believe. It's nothing to trouble you."

"The new King of the Jews. That's what I heard. And men are coming from the East to worship him. The caravan is nearing our beloved city even now."

Aristobolus tried to talk himself into sounding reasonable and authoritative at the same time.

"My lord," he drawled, as though he were talking about something of absolutely no consequence at all, "how long have the people been awaiting the King of the Jews? The so-called King of the Jews, I should say, for are you not already the one and only such king? It is unimportant. Leave it to unimportant people to worry about. Like me!" He ended his little speech with a poor joke, hoping it would deflect his master.

But to his alarm, Herod struggled to his feet. After the Herculean effort he stood swaying for a few moments, fighting for breath, then waddled heavily towards the wall, where he stayed, leaning against it.

"Aristo. Do you take me for a fool? You know what happens to those who take the king for a fool. Do you think I don't know? When a dozen or so of these accursed soothsaying priests have made their way around the desert to get here?"

Aristobolus sighed to himself. The cat was out of the bag and the lord help them all.

"It is true oh far-seeing one. I will find out what is going on. I shall call Ximeno and Eliezer immediately and report to you what they have to say."

"Oh no you don't Aristo, I don't want any of your famous editing. Bring them here. We shall have a meeting. This afternoon." The king waved a dismissive hand and waddled back to his bedchair. Aristobolus stood still, aware of the protocol Herod demanded even of him, his oldest friend, and waited for the king to settle himself.

With an enormous expulsion of breath Herod sank onto the bed, which groaned alarmingly as it took the weight. Aristobolus bowed and took himself silently out, swearing once more under his breath.

Aristobolus, the high priest Ximeno and the chief scribe Eliezer stood at the door to Herod's room, hoping he was asleep. Aristobolus caught Tancred's eye enquiringly. Tancred shook his head. Aristobolus let fly a string of silent oaths and the three of them entered the bedchamber.

Herod had left his bed and arranged himself untidily on a bench placed against the wall, where he leaned his considerable bulk. He looked alarmingly wide-awake. The windows were tightly shut, the summer hot, and the room unbearable with the smell of sweat and disease. Ximeno, who hadn't seen the king for some months, found the bile rising in his throat and disguised his discomfiture with a cough.

"Well?" Herod wasted no time or words.

"Well, your majesty, my understanding is..." Eliezer started but got no further, lapsing into silence at the unwelcome sight of the king pulling himself upright and bearing down on him.

"No weaselling, no wasting words my friend," he said. "Is there another king? What do the scriptures say? What do you say?"

Eliezer gulped. "The prophet Micah has written, my lord, that a new king, the Messiah, shall be born in Bethlehem. From there shall come forth a ruler in Israel'." But of course my lord, we do not know that that is to happen now. It may not be for a thousand years."

Herod, his mountains of fat shaking visibly, towered over the wretched scribe. "And I ask again, what do you say? I hear that men are come to worship this new king. This is now, not in a thousand years."

Eliezer looked across to Ximeno for help. Even Herod was likely to take an easier line with a high priest.

Ximeno said, "Your majesty, I too have heard of these priests from the east who are approaching the city. No-one has spoken to them yet, for they are a day or so away. Might I suggest when they are here that we approach them and ask what exactly has brought them here?"

"Not good enough. Bring them here to me. I would talk with them myself."

Ximeno made another attempt to calm the king. "Might I say, majesty, that this new king, if indeed king he should be, will be but a child? And that the sort of king he would be is a spiritual leader, not a great political and majestic king like your royal self?

" 'A ruler in Israel', that was what the prophet said," thundered Herod. "What is this nonsense about a spiritual leader? A leader is a leader. We already have a leader; he stands before you." Herod was now bellowing downwards onto Ximeno's head, which was bowed, partly from fear, partly to escape the stench which was billowing from the king's mouth.

Herod stood above the priest for a moment, then staggered over to his chairbed and collapsed upon it. His mind was whirling. The child was already born and from what he had heard it was the one thing he had no answer for. This Messiah would be the divine king, the king who the Jews were waiting for, the king who would set them free from Herod's rule.

Oblivious of the great panting sounds that were escaping his lips, Herod tried to think. The child must be stopped; he must never grow to be king. What should be his first move? Who appears to know the most? He must talk to the men from the East. Yes, that must be the way to go about it, find out all there is to find out and then plan accordingly. But be clever about it. Don't make them suspicious. Be friends with them. And then use their knowledge.

"Aristo. Get them here, these priests from the East. Tell them we want to share their understanding and worship with them at this new spiritual leader. Make friends with them Aristo, do you understand my meaning?"

Aristobolus bowed. He understood every word, spoken and unspoken. Together he, Ximeno and Eliezer backed out of the room, glad to have escaped with their lives.

CHAPTER 13

HERODIUM

A mile or so to the north east of Jerusalem a collection of tired and dusty men sat astride their camels and reined them in for a moment. They were at the top of a slight rise, and for the first time they could see clearly their destination. After a hard three months of travel it wasn't a moment too soon. Melchior, the eldest, though made of steel, knew he couldn't go much farther.

Kaeso was sat just slightly behind him and watching the old man with concern. He knew they were approaching a great moment in Melchior's life, something he had lived and prepared for for longer than he could remember, but he also knew he was getting near his seventieth birthday - a prodigious age in those days. Kaeso just hoped and prayed that it all wouldn't be too much for him. It would be the greatest - and most terrible - irony of all if after all the privations of the year Melchoir was not able to enjoy it to the full.

But for the moment at least, Melchoir seemed buoyed up, tired as he was.

No-one spoke; the silence was broken only by the sounds of the camels snuffling and taking a drink from the wide skins that the servants were holding up to them.

Few of them had been to Jerusalem before, and they stared at the grandeur of the buildings stretched out before them. Monuments, towers, palaces, tombs, huge structures which they could not name, walls and gardens, all were laid out like a map drawn in the sand.

"So," said Caspar, "how're we going to do this? We don't all need to see Herod."

"I still think," said Basantor, "we should try and avoid him altogether. I don't see how it can be a secret, the new King of the Jews being born. I'm sure someone can tell us where to go."

Melchior looked at him thoughtfully and repeated himself one last time. "The point is," he said at length, "we don't want to upset him. There's nothing to be gained from being on the wrong side of Herod. If we go about it properly, pay our respects to the king, make no secret of what we are doing, that must be the better way. Secrets always lead to trouble."

Besantor said, "We can't go through that again Melchior. We've agreed, we'll try to avoid him." Melchior shrugged his shoulders. He had tried.

Karsudas, who had been the front rider of the band from the beginning, started up again, waving them on. "We've got to find ourselves somewhere to stay, come what may - let's get on with it."

Several of the Magi had friends or relatives in Jerusalem and they were not expecting much trouble finding lodgings. In any event, they were so used to travelling around the various kingdoms in the east that they were skilled at finding places to stay.

They quickly divided themselves into small groups; Besantor and Caspar both had relatives there and were going to seek them out; Melchior had a great friend from the past he was eager to find again and no doubt stay with; the others would head for the largest inns they could find.

They entered the city through what they later discovered to be the Ginnoth Gate, reined in their beasts again and stared around.

They had entered into the upper city, from where they could look down over the rest rather more easily than they had half an hour earlier. To their left was a palace (later, they discovered it to be Herod's second palace in the city). Lower down, to the right, a much more densely populated area with more palaces and monuments, and what looked like factories. (Again, later they discovered these were perfume factories and a large industrial area.) And in the distance straight ahead something which they guessed was the Antonia - a huge fortress built by Herod to protect the city from the south.

To their immediate left was an area which was clearly more recently built than the rest. Another gateway was visible (the Damascus Gate) and right down to the south of this new area an open space filled with sheep - presumably an animal market.

They started downwards through the straight-lined streets and quickly found themselves in another market place, thronged with people buying and selling. They stopped again to look round, but quickly started to attract attention. It wasn't every day a collection of dusty but clearly well-provided for travellers arrived all at once. As they stood there, one man immediately spoke to them.

"Good day to you my lord travellers. You have travelled far?"

Karsadus, still in the lead and standing at the front, answered, "From Babylon we've come..."

But before he could go further, Hormizdah saw his opportunity and jumped in: "We are seeking he who is born the new King of the Jews. Can you tell us where to find him?"

The man looked puzzled and clearly knew nothing.

The Magi left their horses and camels in charge of their attendants and walked through the market place asking more people. But to their amazement, not one person seemed to know anything about the new King of the Jews. They came together again and were just deciding it was time to give up the quest for the moment and find their lodgings when a handsome stallion approached them with what was evidently a nobleman on its back.

"Men from the East," called the nobleman as he reined his horse in, "do you come seeking the new Kings of the Jews?"

The Magi let Melchior come to the front, who could do little but reply: "Indeed Sir, we do, perhaps you can help us? We have come to worship him and know not where to look."

"I am from the King Herod, and my name is Aristobolus," said the nobleman. "My lord would speak with you and I am to invite you to his palace at Herodium."

The Magi exchanged glances with each other. Any debate about whether or not to tell Herod what they were seeking was now academic. They had to tell all they knew (and tell it as carefully as possible) and gain any help they could. Melchior, at least, was relieved, for he was sure this was the right way to proceed.

"Of course," he replied, "we were planning to visit his Majesty before we left here in any case, and we are delighted to accept his gracious invitation."

"It is some little journey," said Aristobolus, "some eight or nine miles south of the city. Are you ready to travel now? You will of course be the guests of our majesty Herod in his great palace."

Tired as he was, Melchior knew this was more of a command than a suggestion. And in any case, it resolved a number of things at once

- where to stay, where to go next, how to keep on the right side of the King.

"My lord, we shall be delighted to accompany you. Please - lead and show us the way, although you will have to forgive us - we have travelled many miles and our beasts will be a lot slower than your own fine animal."

Aristobolus smiled and turned his horse southwards. "At your own pace travellers," he called, threading his way through the streets towards the Antonia and out through the Tadi Gate.

By the time they arrived at the outskirts of Herodium Melchior and several of the other older Magi were beginning to feel they had done enough for the day. Aristobolus had kept to his word and ambled along at a slow pace, but even so the awkward two-left, two-right legs gait of the camel was taking its toll on Melchior's back. He hoped that the interview with Herod would wait till the following day.

But tired as he was, he could not but be astonished and impressed with the sight of Herodium as it came into view.

The site appeared to be in two halves, the first set in the plain at the end of the half-hour journey from Jerusalem, the second towering above it with gigantic ramparts, castle walls and towers. In the plain itself was a huge pool, 70 metres long, 46 wide and three deep, used apparently both for swimming and a water supply for the fortress above. All around the pool were beautifully sculptured gardens; porticos and ionic columns surrounded the gardens; a pair of halls were built on two of the sides.

There was also a large bathhouse with a number of rooms and heated by a hypocaust system which ran hot air beneath the raised and paved floors which were decorated with mosaics.

But impressive though the gardens, pool and buildings were, they were dwarfed by the fortress and palace itself, constructed on top of a hill, some 60 metres higher.

The Magi stopped and stared. Only Gallio and Yazdegerd had been there before; the others were simply overwhelmed by the sheer scale of the structure.

Aristobolus turned his horse back to them and came to a halt beside Melchior.

"Impressive, eh?"

Melchior nodded in silence.

"It's the spot where his Majesty defeated the Hasmonean and Parthian enemy. And you see the hill itself? And the other one over there?" Aristobolus pointed first up to the hill on which the fortress was built, and then moved his finger towards a second, lower, hill with a flat top a little farther off. As Esther had told Mary many months before, he explained, "We took the apex from that hill and put it on top of this! Can you imagine the work? The number of slaves and craftsmen? And the time it took? But our king was determined to make a fortress and palace together in one place which was unlike any other. What do you think, my friend, do you think he succeeded?"

Before Melchior could answer, Yazdegerd plodded up to them on his camel.

"It is many years since I was last here," he said, "do you not think it is fantastic Melchior? And this is just the outside. You are going to be astonished at what you will see within."

"I think that's my answer," smiled Melchior to Aristobolus. "We have travelled for many months – and many years before that. But never have I seen something like this."

"Let's go inside," said Aristobolus. "The king will see you tomorrow. Today you can rest; tonight we shall have a welcoming party for you. Come, dismount, the slaves will bring everything up."

They hadn't quite realised what lay before them. As the Magi settled their camels and climbed off, they looked up to the fortress and saw a stairway of several hundred steps hewn from stone stretching up and away in front of them.

Aristobolus saw the look on their faces and permitted himself a quiet grin. They would look after the Magi handsomely, but it wouldn't do any harm to wear them out a bit more first. If you were going to try and wheedle information from someone not necessarily on your side, better to have a weak adversary than a strong one. And tonight's abundance of wine would help too.

Slowly they ascended; Melchior and Caspar, the two oldest, lagging behind. As they regained their breath at the top they looked around them and realised the fortress was divided into several parts.

"You see that?" asked Aristobolus, pointing to a small but beautiful building separate from the towers which clearly formed the defensive part of the fortress, "that's Herod's own palace, where you will see him tomorrow. I suggest just a few of you attend the meeting. Tonight you lodge in the eastern tower behind us."

They turned around to take in the sheer size of the tower, huge and completely round, set on a base of solid rock. It stretched up several storeys and Aristobolus led them up even more steps within. Soon they reached a level with a number of rooms opening off, obviously awaiting the travellers.

"I'll leave you here," said Aristobolus, "your things will arrive shortly and you will find all you need. There is refreshment in every room, and I will send for you this evening for the feast. Rest well and get your strength up for tonight!"

The party was long and festive; even the Magi, well experienced at enjoying themselves, woke up the following morning with singing heads.

A servant arrive too early and led the three leaders, Melchior, Caspar and Balthazar, across to Herod's palace. He took them through a long courtyard shaped like a crucifix and on into a great hall, its roof supported by four columns, its floor mosaic tiled, its walls covered with elaborate paintings. At the far end stood a giant throne, before which was arranged a number of chairs in a semi-circle.

"My lords," said the servant, ushering them into the semi-circle. As they walked towards their seats, a door opened behind the throne and Aristobolus entered.

"You are well I trust after the celebrations of last night?" He sounded irritatingly more lively than any of the Magi felt. "Our Majesty will be here before long."

Gallio, who had seen the king so recently, wondered how the others would react when they finally set eyes on the ailing Herod. He also wondered how Herod would actually make his way to the throne; for from what he remembered the king would have the greatest difficulty in moving even a few yards.

A door opened behind them and two further people entered; Aristobolus introduced them as Ximeno the high priest and Eliezer the chief scribe. They now all took their seats and in silence and some trepidation waited the arrival of the king.

CHAPTER 14

THE AUDIENCE

There was a rumbling in the distance beyond the door behind the throne. The sound of shuffling and panting and wheezing and cursing and gasping and swearing. As it got nearer Melchior looked enquiringly over at Aristobolus.

"The king," said Aristobolus simply.

The Magi looked towards the door and waited in silence. The door opened and the servant Tancred came through to hold it back.

There followed three further servants, selected it would seem to be thin enough to slip through the door while supporting the mountain of richly dressed flesh that was breathing out down their necks. They tried not to breathe in.

Two of the servants insinuated themselves round the door and stood within, gently pulling at the garments which surrounded the king like a bell tent. For a moment it looked as though he was not going to make it, and then, with a gargantuan effort, Herod breathed in and was through the door. He stood for a moment, fighting for breath, then pushed the servants aside and made for the throne. It was a journey of no more than twenty feet but it took two or three minutes. It was accompanied by further panting and wheezing. Finally arriving at his destination, the king stood for a moment before the throne while Tancred lined him up with its arms and bowed. Then the king, with a superhuman effort of bravery, allowed himself to fall back into the arms of the throne, which rocked slightly before accepting its burden. Tancred ran to position the royal footstool.

All in the hall were standing throughout this performance; all breathed a sigh of relief when the manoeuvre was accomplished. With a flap of his hand the king indicated they could sit.

The Magi sat down in silence, each trying to subdue their feelings of distaste at the grotesque sight and nose-numbing smells.

Despite the royal garments liberally distributed over the massive figure, bandages could still be seen swelling the enormous limbs; one leg was stuck straight out in front on the footstool, swathed with coarse muslin cloth and covered with grated herbs in a vain attempt to mask the aroma of disease. Balthazar had a worrying feeling he could see small things moving.

There was a moment of relative silence before Herod could summon enough breath to speak. When he did it was evident he was doing his best to be friendly. But even the Magi meeting him for the first time could tell this was not his normal attitude. Wishing to believe the best, each told himself that the illness was to blame.

"My lords," he breathed, "I welcome you to my palace. I trust you are receiving the hospitality so due to travellers. I hope you are refreshed and revived. I hope that the celebrations of last night have not left you with any regrets." This last sentence was clearly a joke, and the king sank back into his throne after the effort of speech and sat while the flesh spontaneously wobbled about him as he chuckled.

Melchior, as leader, got to his feet, summoning the words of protocol: "Your Majesty, my brethren and I thank you from the bottom of our unworthy hearts for your thoughtfulness and kindness. We are indeed revived by your royal hospitality and are honoured to be in your presence".

This was less than the truth and, considering the smell and the sight, they felt less than honoured.

The king nodded graciously and worked up the energy to speak again. "Oh holy priests, what brings you to Jerusalem?"

All knew exactly why they were there, but all had to play the game.

Melchior took a deep breath. There was nothing he could do but speak the truth: "We come, majesty, to seek he who is born King of the Jews, as is foretold by prophets. If indeed that is who it is," he added quickly, in a vague attempt to pacify Herod's suspicions. "We saw his star arise in the east and are come to worship him. But – we do not know where to find him. We are hopeful that your gracious majesty may be able to advise us."

The Magi knew they were living dangerously: disturbing Herod's peace of mind was not recommended. Their hope was that since Herod was clearly trying to be friendly and already knew why they were there, they were probably safe.

Herod tried hard. "There is already a King of the Jews my friends; he is before you." He smiled broadly as he spoke, an intimidating sight.

It was a matter they were prepared for. Caspar stood and replied:

"Your Majesty, this is not a King of the Jews in any sense you might recognise. No-one is seeking to usurp your royal majesty; this is but a child, nothing but a spirit of purity one day to provide spiritual leadership for the Jews."

Everyone in the room knew he was playing with words; there was no room for two Kings of the Jews in any sense. But the game was played on. For the moment.

Herod spoke again. "There is of course the ancient gospel. Eliezer?"

Eliezer, chief scribe, dragged himself to his feet. He too was living on the edge; use the wrong language and his king would not forget.

He had his prompt ready in case he forgot his words. Looking down at a small scroll, he carefully repeated the words he had used to his king earlier: "It is written in our scriptures by the prophet Micah that a new king, the Messiah, shall be born not six miles from here, in a small village called Bethlehem Ephrathah. The prophet said that out of that tiny village would come he who is to be a ruler in Israel. But of course he has not said when this shall come to pass. No-one can know whether such a child has been born or not."

He spoke the last sentence confidently and with all the authority he could muster, hoping he may have deflected the king from his worries and that the Magi would take themselves off and cause no further trouble.

But Herod was not to be put off so easily. He fixed Melchior with a beady eye. "So why are you so sure he is born now?"

Melchior could only repeat what he had said earlier; that they had seen the great light of the stars in the East and believed this to be the sign they had awaited for years. Herod nodded thoughtfully. He tended to agree with Eliezer; this was probably nothing but a flight of fancy on the part of these strange Zoroastrians who seemed to make a habit of trekking around their continent in search of mystical events. But he was not about to risk it.

He spoke again: "Yes, I hear what you say. I understand it is in your nature to follow such portents. And I am sure you are right when you say he is but a child and not a king as I know a king." Herod didn't believe any such thing; he was deeply suspicious and had already decided to track this child down and have it slain. If it were indeed the new King of the Jews, then he had preserved his position. If he were nothing but a simple new born babe - well then, there would be another born tomorrow.

Herod leaned forward; a perilous procedure as Tancred recognised, for he leapt forward to anchor the back of the throne before Herod toppled and then had them all beheaded.

"Oh priests," Herod said, forcing a smile to his lips, "I will join with you in this enterprise. When shall we see the star again?"

Caspar stood. "Your majesty, the star seems to have disappeared. This is indeed why we are so grateful for your help. And of course we had no knowledge such as your esteemed chief scribe here had of the prediction that the child should be born in Bethlehem. Now we know this we shall repair there immediately and make further enquiries."

Herod summoned the strength to wave a hand. Aristobolus, who had remained completely silent and unmoving through the interview, now came forward, bearing a bejewelled purse in his hand.

"Take this with you and present it to the child. If there is a child, of course, and you are convinced it is the one you seek. Take it as a sign of my obeisance to a spiritual leader. And when you have done so, return and tell me all, that I too may travel there and pay royal respects, from one king to another."

The Magi looked at the king and knew not a word of this was to be trusted. At the very least there was no possibility that Herod could be loaded onto a horse or into a coach. They guessed, but didn't know Herod had already decided, that he would despatch a small posse of soldiers to end that small life almost before it had begun.

Herod had decided the audience was over and waved his hand again at his servants who sprang forward to help him to his feet. There followed a few moments of farce as they attempted to get him upright while at the same time trying to avoid breathing in as they did so. It was a race to the finish between standing him upright and them running out of breath. Fortunately for all in the room, Herod was vertical before they fainted.

He had no breath left for further speech. Flapping his hand royally at them in dismissal he shuffled away from the throne and was eased through the door and out of sight.

The Magi, who had all risen to their feet as Herod made his exit, sank back onto their chairs again, releasing sighs of relief.

Arisotobolus stood in front of them: "What further assistance can we give you oh travellers?"

The formal speech was beginning to take over as the audience came to an end. Melchior answered, "Nothing further oh noble one. We are grateful for all your hospitality and help. We shall do as his royal Majesty commands and return with information in due course."

CHAPTER 15

CYRIACUS

Somehow the jackals had got two lambs in the night.

Misael was furious, blaming Acheel, whose watch it had been. Acheel, while perfectly aware it was his fault, didn't want to say so. He put up a spirited defence.

"If Stephanos hadn't been away all day playing at being head of accommodation in Bethlehem I'd have got my proper sleep and been ready for the night."

Stephanos was insulted. "I might remind you Acheel that as a result of my 'head of accommodation' as you put it, we have got just about twice as much money in our pockets as you'd expect at this time of year. And if you can't manage to keep awake when it's your watch you're letting us all down."

Acheel wasn't about to give in.

"Ever since you've decided you've been present at the birth of the next King of the Jews - which I may say no-one else seems to be remotely interested in -"

But Cyriacus interrupted him. "We've had all this Acheel. Just because you won't believe doesn't mean we're all wrong. I know what I heard and saw and I shall believe till the end of my days."

"So why is no-one else interested? I'll tell you why. Because no King of the Jews is going to be born like this downstairs in the animals' quarters in an unknown village at the back of nowhere. Now I'll thank you to be quiet so I can get some sleep."

"Oh no," said Misael, "oh no. There is a lamb to be buried first. One we can eat and give thanks for a better meal than we have had for a month. But the second will not last and needs to be buried. And seeing as it was your watch when it happened I don't see why you should get out of it. Come on, I'll give you a hand."

Acheel didn't reply to this but angrily picked up an axe and a spade and stumped off.

"It's a pity he woke up at all," observed Stephanos dryly. "If he'd stayed asleep the jackals would have taken the lambs away and saved us the trouble of burying them."

"And taken the rest of the flock too once they had the scent of blood," said Misael, "don't be stupid. If you can't think of anything better to do than try and be clever you can come and help us." He set off behind Acheel towards the end of the field to start digging the hard soil.

Stephanos, affronted at being told off, decided to take himself off to find some wood for the fire. He wandered away from the little encampment and followed the track down towards the small wood where he could usually find some fallen branches. He had gone about a quarter of a mile when he noticed a sizable collection of camels, packhorses and walkers slowly making their away along the road from Jerusalem.

Always alert to the chance of business, he changed direction and headed down towards the road. But as soon as he could see the caravan clearly he realised there was not likely to be anything in it for the shepherds. They were far too richly dressed to need the services of his accommodation network. And anyway he knew what rich people thought of shepherds. Even so, perhaps it would be worth a try.

He kept on, ready to turn and run if they seemed aggressive.

"Good day my lords," he called, summoning up as much charm as he could, "I wonder if I can be of any assistance? Do you need any guidance or information? I've lived here for many years, I know everything there is to be known about Bethlehem."

He was right to be wary, however, for Besantor, rode up to him and looked down, scowling. "I know your sort, shepherd. What have you stolen today? Wool or milk? Tools from someone's stable? Lambs even from someone else's flock? Be gone before I chase you away."

Already turned on his heel, Stephanos was about to turn back to the field, when Karsudas rode up beside Besantor and held up a hand.

"Hold on Besantor, it's worth a try." He turned to Stephanos. "Tell me shepherd. Perhaps you are able to advise us. We come seeking he who is born King of the Jews and know not where to look."

Stephanos's jaw fell open. After all his and Cyriacus's attempts to persuade the people of Bethlehem that the new king had been born there had failed, he had fallen into a state of only semi-belief himself. Cyriacus, steadfast as ever, had never wavered and been to visit Ephraim's tiny house every day since the birth. But now, surely, here was proof. If these well-dressed travellers were come to visit the Messiah - surely this must be the truth.

For once Stephanos was tongue-tied. "Yes –" he spluttered, "yes – but – wait – I must go and find someone." There was no way he could handle this himself. And in any event, Cyriacus surely deserved his part in this amazing development; this must be Cyriacus's day. "Wait – please – I will be back in a few moments." And he fled across the fields.

Melchior rode up to Karsudas at the front. "Well," he said, "it looks as though we're getting somewhere at last. Though what our poorly-dressed friend is up to now is anyone's guess."

"Never mind," said Hormizdah, "let's take the opportunity to organise ourselves a little." He dismounted and started to riffle through the bags on his camel, sorting out a clean headscarf for himself. The others followed suit, repacking some of their belongings on the packhorses, taking a drink and a little to eat for themselves and their beasts, walking about and stretching themselves.

Calm as they looked, all were suddenly revived and excited. After the disappointment of finding that no-one in Jerusalem had appeared to know anything and then the disconcerting audience with Herod, their spirits had sunk. Each had lapsed into his own thoughts and secretly begun to wonder whether they had got it all wrong. But now, suddenly, here on the outskirts of Bethlehem, someone knew something. Perhaps it was not a mental mirage after all.

"Here they come," called out Kaeso, relieved to see the two shepherds half-running, half-stumbling across the rough fields towards them.

Cyriacus was beside himself with excitement and thoroughly out of breath; so much so that he could hardly speak. "My lords," he gasped, "we will guide you. It's a privilege for a poor shepherd. Come, come..." Such was his excitement that he waited no longer but started off with his shambling run along the road to the town.

"Wait," called Besantor, attempting to make up for his earlier bad temper, "here – ride with us, there's no need for that..."

But Cyriacus was not listening and hurried on.

"I'll ride," said Stephanos more wisely. He was quite astonished at the offer; usually noblemen like these would keep shepherds at arm's length. He thought they could be priests from their dress, and there was always a chance they might be kindly priests. He was helped up onto one of the pack horses. "It's about three-quarters of a mile. We'll catch him up in a minute; I don't think he'll want to run all the way, however excited he is."

It didn't take long. After galloping from the shepherds' fields down to the road, and then along it towards Bethlehem, Cyriacus suddenly ran out of energy and stopped, panting against a tree.

"Here," said Karsudas, "up there." He pointed to another of the pack horses and Cyriacus gratefully scrambled up. "Come in front with me; show us the way; we have ridden many hundreds of miles and we're grateful for a guide."

"These are bad times," said Caspar, coming up to the front to join them and seeing if he could get a little comfort from a local, "what with the Romans and the Parthians fighting all over the place and Judea in the middle. To say nothing of the brigands and outlaws we've seen on our journeys. What's it like in Bethlehem? Is it safe there?"

Stephanos cautioned himself before he spoke. Who could tell whether these rich people were friends of Herod or not? One word of criticism spoken in the wrong place could get Herod's secret police on the spot within hours and he wouldn't give much for their chances then.

"Well - you have to keep your wits about you," he said carefully. Then he had a thought which seemed pretty safe to him. "Of course, the real danger for noblemen such as yourselves is the desert tribes. You're lucky to have come so far without trouble. They owe allegiance to no-one except themselves."

"Yes, well, we've seen a few in the distance. But we took the precaution to travel with merchant caravans when we could. It made us quite a big number and I think that kept them away."

They were on the outskirts of Bethlehem now and Cyriacus in the lead next to Besantor turned round to call. "Only a few minutes now my lords. The streets are very narrow in the town and the house is beyond, so I'll take you round the outside."

The followed the small road round the little town and went on for a couple of hundred yards.

And then, "We're here," said Cyriacus triumphantly.

The Magi reined their beasts in and stared in puzzlement. All they could see was a tumbledown building that looked little more than a cave beside the road. Two hens were standing in the doorway and a small donkey was tethered outside. An elderly man dressed in what looked like a pile of thin blankets was lolling against the wall and smoking some kind of pipe which was belching out evil smoke. Seeing the Magi come to a halt outside his house and recognising Stephanos and Cyriacus, Ephraim sprang to his feet.

Besantor turned to look at Cyriacus. "This is it?" he asked incredulously. "This is where the King of the Jews is born? But..."

He stared about him and looked to Melchior. None of them had known exactly what to expect, but it certainly wasn't this. It wasn't just the humbleness of the house; it was the fact that no-one was there. They had anticipated crowds; they had found no-one. As puzzled as any of them, Melchior felt it was up to him as leader to try to understand.

He looked across at Cyriacus. "Tell me, my friend," he said in as calm a voice as he could manage, "on what grounds do you believe the King of the Jews is born here? It is hard to believe."

Cyriacus would normally have been overwhelmed at being cross-questioned by such noble people. But he knew what he believed and was ready to defend himself.

"We saw the angel..." he started, and recounted the vision he had seen in the fields a few days earlier.

Then Stephanos also spoke up. "And the midwife Salome. When she delivered the baby she said she had seen a wonderful thing. That that day salvation was born to Israel."

"Yes," came in Cyriacus eagerly, gathering confidence, "and Joseph, the baby's father, said he's the son of God."

The Magi started to divide amongst themselves. Yazdegerd and Perozadh, two who usually maintained a respectful silence in front of their leaders - and in front of Melchior in particular, given his age - exchanged glances. Yazdegerd spoke first, looking at Melchior.

"Old friend, I cannot believe in this. Are we expected to take this shepherd's word for it that the King of the Jews, whom we have travelled so far to find and pay homage to, is actually living in this...this...*cave?*"

Perozadh said, "And what about our gifts? They must represent riches beyond belief to such peasants. Do you really believe we should simply leave them here to be squandered?"

Melchior found himself in a quandary. He could understand and sympathise with every word the two had said. Perhaps it was time for a top-level meeting. "Caspar. Balthazar. Let us talk quietly for a while."

The three of them dismounted and walked a few paces away. Some of the others dismounted too and stretched their legs. A few curious passers-by gathered, staring in astonishment at the richness of the camels' livery and the servants standing around with the packhorses laden with the baggage of long journey.

Then Balthazar had a good idea. "Our gifts - we treat them as a test. We know that gold represents earthly kingship; that myrhh is for a physician; that incense is for the divine. We offer our gifts and we will know from what is chosen what the child is to be."

Caspar laughed. "And what if the father takes all three?"

"No-one would take all three. That would be greed on a grand scale. That is not how things are."

Melchior, who had been quiet so far, now spoke with the voice of authority. "I think we should go in. We can put Balthazar's idea to the test. It doesn't really matter whether the father takes all three or not; we will know from his response which really appears to matter to him. And in any case I believe that we shall know when we see the child. Everything we have done over the last months has led us to this. We have journeyed dangerously, spoken with the king appointed by Rome, travelled with the humblest of God's men. We must not fail now. Let us have the courage to face this last hurdle. Come. I will go in. Follow me."

Whether he was as sure of himself as he sounded the other Magi would never know. But Melchior was behaving as a leader should; he waited no longer and strode purposefully towards Ephraim's tiny dwelling. After a moment's hesitation, the others started to follow him.

But just for a moment Besantor stayed back. He had travelled in the front of the convoy with Cyriacus and had recognised the true belief in the shepherd.

"Thank you my friend," he said. "Your God will not forget your steadfastness."

Besantor followed the others to the door, leaving Cyriacus looking after him with tears in his eyes.

CHAPTER 16

AT THE MANGER

Unaware of what was happening outside, Mary and Joseph were going about their duties as new parents. It was easier for Joseph, with the experience of two other children behind him and, of course, he was perfectly fit.

For Mary it was a different matter. Now just seventeen and strong, she had recovered well from the birth. But she was a slim girl and, after a fortnight, she still had to move carefully. And she was quite overwhelmed by the whole idea of parenthood; of the small noisy body totally reliant on her. The sense of responsibility had taken her by surprise. It simply hadn't struck her that once the excitement of the birth was past, as every new mother was to realise, everything depended on her.

Joseph's relations and such new friends as they had gained still visited, but the visits were becoming fewer. Cyriacus the shepherd, the godfather, came every day, the one constant reminder of that other question that ebbed and flowed in their minds: was Jesus really the Son of God?

The new parents had put the matter to one side. There was enough to do simply caring for the tiny new child and neither felt like raising it again. In their sleep-deprived state, they did not know what to think. Mary veered between deciding it was all nonsense brought on by a few dreams and the hormone-related euphoria of being pregnant - and the memory of conversations with Elizabeth, her vision in the night, the message of the shepherds, the meetings in the temple.

It was simply too big a problem and she had shut it away.

There was plenty to do. Joseph, a dutiful and experienced father, did all he could to help in the tiny room that was their home. Money was short, but he found himself a few jobs around the town and managed to earn enough for them to eat. And he found a good friend in Ephraim, who assured them there was no need to hurry back to Nazareth until Mary was fully fit. And like Mary, Joseph too had tried to put the problem to the back of his mind.

Stephanos hadn't stayed while the Magi debated whether to go in or not. Having met the travellers he had finally decided Cyriacus was right; this was the Messiah. There's no-one more fervent than a convert and Stephanos was determined to get Misael and Acheel down here straightaway to see for themselves, even if it meant missing the fun himself while he guarded the flocks.

To be truthful he'd had enough running for the day already but he forced himself on and up the hillside to the small encampment. Misael was tending the fire; Acheel nowhere to be seen.

"Misael," gasped Stephanos, collapsing in front of the fire and promptly getting a cloud of smoke from a damp branch in his eye, "it's true, it's true, you must go," he coughed. "You and Acheel, you must go."

In face of this elliptical cry, Misael looked steadily at Stephanos. "I know you're busy being the businessman and haven't got much time to spare, but we're not mind-readers. Can you spare a moment to tell me what you're talking about?"

The sarcasm was wasted on Stephanos who was too full of everything.

"The noblemen - I think they might be priests - come a long way. Come to see the new King. You've got to go, you and Acheel. Perhaps you'll believe then. Oh thank you Lord on high, thank you for showing me your Son." Stephanos was by now on his knees, staring heavenwards.

Misael dropped his sarcasm; this appeared to be serious.

"Slowly friend. Who are these noblemen? And what exactly did they say?"

"They're noblemen, from the east I think. They said they're come to see he who is born King of the Jews. We - Cyriacus and me - took them there - they're at Ephraim's house. You must go. You and Acheel."

"Acheel!" called out Misael, "here." Then he gave Stephanos a piercing look. "And you'd better be right..."

"I am, I am right." Stephanos looked affronted. Misael looked at him and felt he had to believe him. Even Stephanos couldn't put up this sort of show without some justification.

Acheel appeared and cocked a questioning eye at Misael.

"Come with me," said Misael. "Stephanos and Cyriacus believe they've got some real proof that little Jesus is the Son of God. Yes - I know..." Acheel had put his bored disbelieving face on again. "But give them a chance. Look at him." Stephanos was still on his knees. " Stephanos - you've got to stay here with the flocks. We'll see you later. Come Acheel, let's go."

Even Acheel, cynic though he was, couldn't bring himself to say no to this and they hurried off together. Stephanos crouched down by the fire, sadness at not being at Ephraim's house easily outweighed by the excitement of finally believing.

As Melchior ducked under the low doorway of Ephraim's house, he at first thought he was going to see nothing at all, so dark was it in the tiny room. And as Balthazar and Caspar crowded in too it got even darker. But slowly he could make out the scene: baby in manger by the wall, mother sitting next to it, father standing by the side. And on the floor all around a motley collection of chickens, a goat and a lamb.

Joseph looked up in astonishment as the room was filled. Mary, bending down to the child, realised the room had got darker and turned round to the door, equally amazed to see these important looking people crowding around her.

Aware of the shock their arrival must cause, Melchior spoke gently. "Do not be alarmed. We are from the East - we have come to find and worship the Son of God," he said as he stared down at the tiny child lying amongst the straw in the trough. And then, before he could stop himself, "Is this truly He? Is this the Messiah, the saviour of the Jews?"

Melchior could not have known what a difficult question he had asked. He could not have guessed how confused Mary and Joseph themselves were. And yet, even by speaking those words, he was helping them to believe.

Joseph glanced down at Mary and then said, "My wife had a dream and she was visited in the dream by an angel of the Lord, who said, 'You shall bring forth a son and he will be great and called the Son of the Highest and the Lord God shall give him the throne of his forefather, David. That holy child you shall bear shall be called the Son of God' ".

It was enough for Melchior and the others. They sank to their knees. Joseph turned to Mary; their eyes met and for them the question was finally answered. They knew and would believe for ever that their son Jesus was indeed the Son of God. For just one blinding, astounding, moment they felt themselves not to be in the room at all, but joined with their newborn son and their Lord God in some kind of mystical holy union which was above and beyond this world.

The silence of prayer and unspoken thought should have been unbroken for minutes; but it had lasted no more than seconds before it was interrupted by a scuffle at the doorway.

Determined not to miss this moment, Acheel, Misael and Cyriacus had somehow managed to push their way through the small crowd of Magi and their servants standing outside Ephraim's house. Despite the glances of disapproval to be expected from the noble rich to the bedraggled poor, the shepherds wriggled their way to the front, eager to demonstrate their familiarity with the family, finally recognised by the world.

"At last...the Son of God!" Acheel, the unbeliever, spoke up unashamedly.

Misael kicked him. He didn't know exactly why he kicked him, except that he had a faint feeling that he really couldn't allow Acheel to take centre stage like this, after all his cynicism.

"My lords," Misael said to the Magi, still on their knees, "we should join you in thanksgiving." He kicked Acheel again and pulled him down to the floor, where the pair of them lined up with Melchior and the two others.

Acheel looked out of the corner of his eye at the worshippers and stayed in position until Melchior sat up and clambered to his feet.

Melchior bowed to the small family group and found he didn't know what to say. After preparing for years and travelling for months he hadn't expected quite such a humble finale. But what had he expected? He didn't really know, but had somehow thought that the next step would take care of itself. Instead he found himself in a tiny room in a tiny house with seemingly nothing about to happen next.

Apart from Joseph's description of Mary's dream very little had been said. Mary hadn't opened her lips; even the baby was asleep and silent.

Melchior looked round for inspiration. Caspar coughed. "Perhaps we might let some of our other brethren in? And make some more room?" Caspar looked hard at the shepherds as he said this.

"Of course," said Melchior in relief. "Let them come in. And we are very grateful to you, shepherd," he added speaking directly to Cyriacus.

Misael and Acheel stood up; they knew a dismissal when they heard it. They also felt slightly hard done by. After all, it was they who had first helped Mary and Joseph; it was Stephanos and Cyriacus who had led the Magi to the birth place.

Misael was too proud. Acheel wasn't. He followed Melchior out of the house and stood looking hard at him outside.

"We're glad to have been of service to you, lords of the East." He stood still and continued to look hard at Melchior, recognising him as the leader. "It's hard on the hills at this time of year," he added, in case Melchior hadn't got the point. "But we're always ready to help, in addition to everything we do for the sheep. And others."

Melchior nodded towards Besantor, who kept the joint purse.

"Oh," said Acheel, rapidly transferring his attentions and crossing quickly to Besantor. "My lord?"

Besantor found some coins and held them out to Acheel. Apparently it was not quite enough, for Acheel took them and stood his ground. Misael moved away, embarrassed, while at the same time hoping Acheel would be successful, for they always needed the money.

"Of course," said Besantor, adding a few more coins, deciding that enough was enough and that this had better be sufficient. It was; Acheel bowed and backed away, joining with Misael in saying final farewells and hurrying back towards the hills. They had quite forgotten Cyriacus, who had somehow managed to remain behind in the corner of the room. And Mary and Joseph had got so used to seeing him there that they barely noticed him.

Others of the Magi had by now crowded in and were paying their respects.

The three leaders waited outside and debated what to do next. They had yet to present their gifts and assess the reactions.

"This is difficult," said Balthazar. "Are we really convinced by this?"

Melchior looked shocked. "I'm convinced. Aren't you? I thought we all were."

At the Manger

Balthazar shrugged. "I just don't know. Is this what you expected?" Unconsciously he had echoed Melichior's own thoughts of just a few moments ago. He went on, "It's one thing to give thanks for the birth of a new child - who might or might not be the Son of God - and perhaps we shall never know. But to leave these costly gifts... Well, I'm just not sure."

"Caspar?" asked Melchior, lost.

Although Melchior was by common consent the leader, there had often been moments when it was Caspar who provided the final authoritative judgement on a problem. He had already come to his conclusion.

"Yes - it's difficult. But we've seen the signs and invested so much in this and come so far. We've seen parents who believe and even shepherds who believe. Shepherds! If such as they can, we can. Let us have the courage of our convictions. I believe the Son of God has been born here, even if it's not quite what we expected and not the son of the God we worship. But then, what right did we have to expect anything? Who could say that God would do what we would expect? We came to pay our respects, and, if we're honest, to protect ourselves for the future. We know what people used to think of us, the poor reputation we had - and still do have in some quarters. It's in our interests to pay homage here and be seen to do so. We don't need to go as far as worship. I vote we go in and get on with it. After all, what will we have lost? Three expensive presents. We can afford it. And what do we stand to gain? A big fillip to our reputation if this is the new King of the Jews. I say we go forward."

Melchior clapped his childhood friend on the back. "Well said Caspar; as ever able to find your way to the heart of a problem. Come Balthazar. Get the gifts and let us go inside."

They each found one of the three gifts and pushed their way through the crowd that was growing every moment. Even Balthazar, the doubter, began to feel comforted by the excitement of the people.

The Magi inside gave way to their leaders, as many as possible managing to stay in the little room.

Melchior took the lead, speaking directly to the child who had now awoken and was staring around the room in the unfocused way of new born babies. "Oh Holy Child, we are here to pay homage to

127

the new-born King of the Jews. And we bring gifts to match the occasion. I humbly offer you the gift of gold: a gift that befits the birth of a king on earth." He laid the gold thurible down in the straw before the child.

Caspar then stepped forward. "I bring you the gift of frankinsense: a gift that befits the birth of a divine being."

And then Balthazar, holding the casket of myrrh. "I bring you the gift of myrrh: a gift that befits the birth of a healer for his faith."

The three Magi stepped back, bowed, and waited for a response.

Then, for the first time, Mary spoke. Only an hour earlier she had still been undecided, her thoughts in turmoil, one moment believing that her son was indeed the Messiah, the next dismissing the idea as preposterous. But now, like the Magi themselves, she began to be sure of herself. This beautiful pure child quietly awake before her was the Son of God.

Her knowledge of the writings of the scriptures helped her form her words. "My lords," she said, "we thank you for your words and gifts, so carefully chosen. There will be many years before my Son claims his place at the right hand of God. For now, your gifts will represent everything He shall stand for." She said no more but bent down to tend to her son.

The three Magi looked at each other. Mary had said so little, but in accepting all three of the gifts had said everything.

"There is something else," said Melchior after a moment. "We have another gift for your Son. We have come straight from King Herod's palace and he sends this in praise and thanksgiving." He held out the bejewelled purse full of gold coins which Aristobolus had handed him at Herodium.

"The king?" said Joseph, in both astonishment and alarm. "He knows? About this?" He waved his hand towards Mary and the child, quite unsure how to react. "He has sent us gold? But why?"

Melchior was in as much difficulty as Joseph. He couldn't tell him what he really thought about Herod, nor how much danger he guessed he might be in. It was, after all, just speculation. And he didn't want to endanger himself and the other Magi by unguarded words spoken in public. He decided not to answer directly.

"Gold is always useful; it will be money when you really need it.

Take it and give thanks. And beware." That was as far as he felt he could go.

Joseph took the purse uncertainly, glancing across at Mary. She had opted out; this was man's work and not for her. "I thank you, noblemen from the east," Joseph said at last. "I thank you for everything you've said and brought today. May the Lord be with you."

It was the end; Melchior, Balthazar and Caspar backed out to join their comrades. Among the group of travellers there was a sense of anti-climax. They had come so far, found a birth which no-one seemed particularly interested in, spent no more than a few minutes with the parents and child, and now it was all over. And Babylon seemed a long way away.

Inside, with just Cyriacus and Ephraim for company, Mary and Joseph looked at each other. Along with what for them was the final confirmation, had come something quite different; a thought neither of them had confronted before. If the existing King of the Jews was showing interest in their son, where did that leave them? Without exactly knowing why, both were frightened.

CHAPTER 17

SLAUGHTER

Stephanos had let the fire go out, an unforgivable thing to do.

He was keeping less than half an eye on the sheep; all his concentration was directed towards the little town of Bethlehem down and away to the north, where he was trying to envisage what was happening in Ephraim's house.

He was bursting with excitement. He would never know how he had managed to make himself stay behind and let the others share the experience of seeing the rich travellers arrive at Jesus's birthplace. For the time being he was just hopping from one foot to the other and holding his breath till the others returned.

When they did, smiles all over their faces, they didn't even trouble to complain about the fire.

Cyriacus could not contain himself, despite being out of breath from the effort of catching the others up. "If you could have seen it Stephanos..."

Stephanos, who would like to have seen it above all things, shouted, "Get on with it."

"...oh...oh..."

That appeared to be all that Cyriacus could manage so Stephanos turned to Misael.

"It was truly wonderful. Those travellers, they looked like kings in that tiny room. And Mary and Joseph, they were so...dignified. You knew, *knew*, they were the parents of the Messiah. And the baby Jesus. He was so good."

"And they brought presents – such presents, such rich things." Even Acheel had become enthusiastic, his past scepticism quite behind him. He absentmindedly put some wood on the dead fire, still smiling at the memory.

"Are they still there?" demanded Stephanos, thinking he might rush back himself for a final look.

"They were when we left," said Cyriacus, finding his voice again, "but I don't know for how long."

"Right," shouted out Stephanos, hurtling off down the hill, "I've had an idea..."

"Oh no," said Misael.

The Magi had clambered up on their camels, the servants had got the packhorses in line, the crowd had got bigger.

Inside Ephraim's house the scene looked unchanged, except for the three gifts lying where they had been put, in the straw before the baby's sleeping place. Mary and Joseph had not exchanged a word since the Magi had gone back outside, each too busy with their thoughts and the enormity of it all.

Besantor was just about to lead off when he and Caspar, next to him at the front, were suddenly aware of a wild collection of blankets blowing along the street towards them. It was Stephanos, hair and clothing flying in the wind.

"My masters," he gasped as he arrived, "may I perhaps be of one last service to you?"

"Of course," said Caspar, wondering how much money Stephanos would want this time.

"It's just a service," said Stephanos, appearing to read his mind and attempting to put it at rest. "I just thought your lordships might want somewhere to stay the night? I know where the best caravansarai are around here."

"Thank you my friend," said Balthazar, "but we are bound back to Herodium in Jerusalem. We must talk to the king. I've no doubt he will provide us with accommodation, as he did last night."

"The king?" repeated Stephanos in surprise. He did not know exactly why, but he felt this was not right.

Sensing the question in his voice and already wondering within themselves how wise this was, the Magi exchanged glances.

Melchior came to the front. "You sound surprised shepherd," he said, wondering whether from this simple mind might come a view on the question facing them all.

"Well," said Stephanos slowly, feeling this was all beyond him, "we...all of us...have wondered what the King of the Jews might think about another King of the Jews..." He allowed his voice to trail off, not at all sure how far he should go with these rich travellers. He still didn't know how friendly they were with King Herod.

Melchior looked across at Caspar, and then at Balthazar.

Caspar took it upon himself to answer, looking first at the other Magi and then back to Stephanos. He chose his words carefully; he too didn't know how much he should say outright; Herod's spies could be anywhere, even in this small gathering outside Ephraim's house.

"We could leave it for a day or so while we prepare for our journey back to Babylon," he said, feeling this was safe enough, while at the same time leaving them room for negotiation later.

Stephanos was satisfied with this; instinctively he knew he had gone as far as he could dare.

"I will lead you to the nearest caravansary, my lords, it is about two miles back on one of the great routes across Israel. You would never find it for yourselves." He added the last as a bit of window-dressing. Both he and they knew all about trade routes and where caravansarais were. But he never gave up; there was bound to be something in it for him, even without asking.

He did well out of it, and returned to the camp with a pocket full of shekels.

For the Magi it was a welcome rest away from the politics of Herod's court. Stephanos had done no more than reinforce what many of them had been thinking. Here at least was the opportunity to take stock and decide what to do. And they were tired. Buoyed up by the excitement of arriving at Jerusalem, the meeting with Herod, and then the serene moments with Mary and Joseph and the child, they had forgotten how much they had done over the past few days. But once they stopped, with no immediate pressures upon them, they knew they were exhausted - the young Magi just as much as Melchior and the other older ones.

In fact Stephanos had been a real help. He had led them straight to one of the better establishments, and one that he knew was not so busy as most. All the travellers were accommodated; all went to bed early and all but one slept soundly.

The exception was Caspar. The words of Stephanos and the worry they all had about Herod whirled around inside his head and he could not get to rest. In that strange world halfway between sleep and wakefulness he found himself in conversation with someone he didn't know at all but felt he had to pay full attention to.

"So my travelling friend. You are thinking of returning to King Herod and telling him what you have found and where you have found it."

"We think we are," said Caspar, quite unsure of himself.

"And you think this is wise? You know what the king is. Especially these days when he is not himself."

"We have talked about it..." said Caspar, a little weakly.

"You should not do this," said the unknown man. "You will be endangering not just yourselves, but the mother and father and the child too. Go another way. Return home as fast as you can and try not to draw attention to yourselves. Go quickly and quietly."

Caspar was awake and not awake at the same time. He didn't know when he had begun talking to this man and he didn't know when he ended. He didn't know whether it was a dream or simply a debate he was having with himself, or just a rerun of exchanges he and the other Magi had already had. All he did know for certain when he was finally wide awake was that they must avoid Herod at all costs. And he had no trouble persuading the others, for many of them had come to the same conclusion themselves.

They set off early the following morning. Stephanos had already told them the way to a route that would avoid Jerusalem. By seven o'clock they were on their camels and plodding north-eastwards, hoping to put many miles between themselves and Herod before he would realise they were not coming back.

It was two days before he did realise. But something else was happening too. And he was incandescent with fury.

"Aristobolus!" he bellowed, "ARISTOBOLUS"

Outside Herod's door Tancred shivered in terror. Aristobolus was not there; Tancred did not know where he was; and was therefore now probably facing death. You did not survive such a rage with Herod if it could conceivably be your fault.

"TANCRED." Herod had transferred his wrath to the one person he knew would always be there.

Tancred entered, bowing to the floor in the vain hope this would deflect Herod's fury. "Master, your Majesty, Excellency, Sire?" He uttered every word of subservience he could think of.

Herod was lying prone on his bed. "Here. Up," he roared. Tancred crept across the room and attempted the near impossible job of propping his master up against pillows quite unequal to the task. "UP

UP UP," screamed Herod. Tancred tugged and pushed, aware that he was damned if he failed to get Herod up, and damned if he hurt him in so doing. In fact, he was damned.

"Where's Aristobolus?" demanded Herod, once he was vaguely sitting vertically.

"He's not here, Majesty, Excellency," said the wretched Tancred. "I will send to find him if your Majesty wishes."

"Of course his Majesty wishes, why else would I be asking for him, imbecile? Find him. Tell him I want him here immediately. And send two guards in."

Tancred scuttled from the room.

The guards entered fearfully. Reports of Herod's rage were sweeping down the corridors.

"Follow that fool Tancred. When he has found the lord Aristobolus and sent him to me, take him and slay him."

"Sire." The two guards backed out of the room as fast as they could. The fate of Tancred meant nothing to them. Their own fate certainly did and the more space they could put between themselves and their maddened king the better.

Herod lay on his bed, puffing, until Aristobolus entered.

"Where've you been Aristo?" the king growled. "I needed you."

Aristobolus thought quickly; what answer might save his life? "I have heard, oh master, there is a new-found herb which alleviates the symptoms of extreme pain and I was consulting the royal herbalist to command him to order a large quantity for your royal person."

Fortunately Herod wasn't listening to this nonsense; he had too much to worry about. "Cullinane was here yesterday. He has heard rumours. What can you tell me?"

Aristobolus cursed inwardly. He knew exactly what General Cullinane was referring too and knew very well that the outcome was going to be catastrophic. In fact, that was precisely why he had tried to be unavailable this morning. Unless he very much misread the situation they were all facing a period of terrible upheaval.

He didn't know how to begin.

"My lord..." he faltered.

"All right, if you can't tell me I'll tell you." Herod directed such a terrible look at Aristobolus that he felt his heart lurch. This was going to be even worse than he had supposed. "Is it not true that some of my cursed family are already rejoicing? Is it not true that they believe that Herod the Great is already dead? Is it not true that they are already making plans for succession? Is it not true that my own family is not to be trusted and that my oldest adviser Aristo has failed me in not warning me of this outrage?"

Unfortunately every word was true and Aristobolus knew he was dead from that moment. He bowed his head in silence. Herod's younger family was no more stable than Herod himself. Herod was hated by them and somehow the word had got around that he was dead. The rejoicing had started immediately and the hierarchy of the new court already decided upon. It was just regrettable that the word had been false.

"And there's another thing. What happened to those infidels from the East?"

Aristobolus had been wondering the same thing. It was not his fault that the Magi hadn't come back but it was certainly going to seem like it. Not only that: Herod was going to say, rightly, that he should have sent spies to watch the men from the East.

"I do not know, majesty. Perhaps they are still with the child." It was a lame answer, but Aristobolus's mind was fading. The end was here. Everyone knew how it was when you worked with Herod. It always ended in failure.

"Guards!" Herod's word barked out; six guards entered immediately. "Take him. Destroy him."

"My lord.." But Herod was already looking away, planning his next move. The guards took the unfortunate Aristobolus away, weeping as he went.

"Servant!" Herod could not think of the name of the next man outside. The man came in at a rush, knowing that anything less would mean death for him too. Herod bellowed: "Bring me General Cullinane."

"Sire," the servant said, backing away as quickly as he decently could. He had no idea where to find General Cullinane but was not going to say so; he desperately hoped he could find someone who would know. But with both Arisbolus and Tancred now gone lines of command and information were hopelessly blurred.

But he had not got away with it yet. "Servant!" barked out Herod again, and the wretched man came back to face his master. "You can find me Tarphon as well."

The servant now had two people to find and no idea where to look. He didn't even know who Tarphon was.

Outside Herod's bedchamber the quivering servant started asking questions of anyone he could find. The third person he spoke to came to his rescue. Tarphon, it appeared, was one of Aristobolus's men and was to be found across the courtyard. The servant scampered across, hoping firstly that Tarphon would be there and that secondly he would know where General Cullinane might be found. Miraculously he was in luck, and within ten minutes both were standing before the king.

"Tarphon," said Herod, "the traitor Aristobolus is dead. You will replace him. You will never move from beyond this door without my permission. Cullinane, you and I will plan to put down this infamous insurrection against my royal person. I have made a list of the junior members of my family. They will all be found and all put to death. But that is not all. While you are about it, send a cohort to Bethlehem and kill every boy child that has been born there in the last two years. We are going to clear our royal court of all existing traitors and all future pretenders to my throne. Return here when this is done. Return here by tomorrow. Go Cullinane. Tarphon, I will speak further with you, for there is much to do. Herod the Great will be the Great for many years to come and that is what we shall ensure."

The General left the room clutching Herod's piece of parchment, staring at the list of his sons, nephews and other relations. It was not to his taste, this wholesale slaughter. And as for all the innocent babies – he knew that Herod was not only mortally ill but becoming insane as well. He also knew that if he didn't follow instructions, he would be following Aristobolus to his death.

Tarphon felt sick with dread. It was the last sort of promotion he wanted. But as with General Cullinane, the alternative was even worse.

CHAPTER 18

DANGER

Kentius listened to General Cullinane's speech with incredulity. However much the general might have been appalled at Herod's instructions, as a good senior officer he knew how to keep his opinions to himself and carry out his duties.

Kentius, on the other hand, had no such responsibilities. He was already thoroughly fed up with this posting; he had been based in Jerusalem for four years now and was impatient to get back to his wife Anna and their children Jilius and Rufus in Radlium just outside Rome. He hadn't made much secret of this and his fellow soldiers thought he was living dangerously. Herod's informers were very active in the army and it could only be a matter of time before his treasonable views would bring about an early death. Perhaps that was why he wanted so much to get back to Rome.

He also kept what to his colleagues in the army were some strange friends. He was apt to frequent the temple; as the holy of holies for the Jews, Romans were not exactly common visitors there. But Kentius had a curiously scholarly outlook on life for a soldier. Not remotely religious himself, he was nonetheless fascinated by religion itself and all the various forms it could take. He had got to know teachers for their learning and priests for their beliefs. Perhaps he was looking for the comfort of religion himself and hoping that some day an astonishing or revealing fact would present itself and that that would be a turning point in his life.

He had got to know Zacharias, priest in the temple, husband of Elizabeth, father of the boy John. He knew of Elizabeth's cousin Mary, knew they were living in Bethlehem, knew of the birth of the baby Jesus. But he knew no more than that. Zacharias had been careful never to reveal to his army friend the circumstances surrounding the birth. It was easy to predict Herod's reaction to the birth of the new King of the Jews and Zacharias was not going to be responsible.

But Kentius had remembered the connection and was determined to tell Zacharias of the danger the baby was in in Bethlehem. There was little time to waste; his cohort was to be despatched later in the day and he could only snatch half an hour away from the barracks. Even that was a risky procedure, for the centurions were busy planning the day's evil works and were scurrying everywhere.

Asking a friend to cover for him if necessary, he slipped out of his quarters and tried to hurry unobtrusively to the temple. He knew where to find Zacharias and knew him well enough to be confident he would come out to talk for a moment privately.

The priest was surprised to see his friend at a time when he would expect him to be on army duties but could see the urgency in his face.

"My friend, you have something to tell me?" Zacharias already knew danger was in the air; the whole of Jerusalem had heard that Herod was on the rampage and all were fearing the consequences.

Kentius told him what he knew and that his cousins in Bethlehem were in terrible danger. And then he said, "Priest, my friend, I must go immediately. There is danger everywhere and I must get back. I will try to see you soon; but get word to your cousins as fast as you can - you have no more than a day to get them away".

Zacharias blessed him and clasped him warmly around the shoulders before hurrying away to find a messenger.

Kentius ran back the way he had come as fast as he could.

When he arrived at the barracks they were waiting for him. Within half an hour he was dead.

Zacharias knew that he too was being watched. But it was easier for him. As a priest he was always talking to people and it was simple enough to find a messenger who would hurry to Bethlehem. He gave careful instructions, including the vital need to be as unobtrusive as possible. He also handed over a small package to give to Joseph.

In Bethlehem, two days after the visit of the Magi, Mary and Joseph had no idea they were in imminent danger. None of the Magi had alerted them, being more concerned with their own problem. No rumour of Herod's latest madness had reached them and they were planning to start their journey back to Nazareth within a few days. They were worried about Menci; the little donkey, faithful friend, was looking older and losing weight. They were in two minds about whether to try to find a younger animal for the return journey and had already asked Ephraim to see if he could find something for them.

Life had become quiet again for Mary and Joseph. No more callers had come after the Magi. Cyriacus had maintained his daily visit but the other shepherds were too busy preparing the flocks and barns for the winter. Doubts and uncertainties had risen again. No-one knew what sort of life the Son of God should expect to lead on earth and memories fade fast. Without any further signs it was already increasingly difficult to believe that this was anything other than a very special child. But then weren't all children very special to their parents?

They went to bed early. Winter was nearly here and the nights were already long and cold. They preserved their small supplies by covering themselves with sheepskins and keeping the baby child well wrapped in his swaddling clothes. They were grateful for the presence of Menci with them in the tiny room, adding his own warmth to that of the small fire.

It was all the more unusual therefore to hear a knocking at the doorway in the dark when all were asleep.

Joseph sat up alarmed; he had nothing to worry about that he knew, but such a happening was always a cause for concern.

He picked up a nearby crook, left behind by Cyriacus, and quietly moved to the doorway. Mary was still asleep and Joseph tried not to disturb her.

"Yes?" he said quietly without moving the wooden planking away from the doorway.

"Joseph? I have important news from Zacharias. I must tell you immediately."

Hearing the urgency in the man's voice, Joseph pulled the planking to one side and welcomed him in. They stood facing each other across the light from the fire. Mary had by now awoken and was sitting up, the bedclothes pulled tightly around her.

"There is grave news in Jerusalem. The priest Zacharias said I must tell you immediately. You are in great danger. A cohort of Roman soldiers will be here tomorrow with orders to kill all young children. You must leave immediately. Zacharias suggests you make for the west, to Alexandria perhaps, beyond the realms of the king."

"But why?" Joseph was reeling from the news; half asleep he was

THE HOUSE OF BREAD

again not making the connection between his son and the threat the new leader of the Jews would be to Herod.

Zacharias, wise as ever, had given nothing away to the messenger beyond the bare need to get Joseph's family away from Bethlehem.

"I know not," said the messenger, "but I bring you this from the priest. He said you would need it for the journey."

Joseph opened the package, to find it containing money.

He blessed the priest silently for his thoughtfulness and also for the great sacrifice he must have made. A priest in the temple made little money and needed every shekel he could get. But of course Zacharias had no knowledge of the gold Herod had already sent; no knowledge that money was no longer a problem for them. He showed the contents of the package to Mary. "How can we ever repay?" he asked. "We cannot send it back and hurt Zacharias."

"I have an idea," she said in reply, and whispered to him. He looked back for a moment, a smile breaking across his worried face as he realised what a good idea it was.

"Please wait," he said to the messenger, "there is something for you to take back to our cousin."

He burrowed amongst their few belongings in the corner of the room, found the bag of frankincense that Caspar had given them and took some from it. Wrapping it in large green leaves and tying with gut, he handed the package over to the messenger.

"For Zacharias. Tell him we thank him from the bottom of our hearts and that he should sell this to the temple seniors. He will understand. And thank you too my friend. Can we offer you something before your journey?"

"No," said the messenger. "I must get back as fast as I can. It is a dangerous time and the sooner I am back in Jerusalem the better. I bid you farewell. And you my lady. And you little child; God save you."

"Farewell to you," said Joseph. "And may God travel with you."

With the messenger gone, Joseph turned back to Mary. "We have little time to waste," he said, "we must be gone at first light. And Zacharias is right about Alexandria; it is well away from Herod and I have family there. We can disappear into the crowds there and I am sure I can get work."

"But why? Why is all this?" asked Mary, still wondering if she was dreaming.

"Do you not understand? We should have realised. Herod is never going to welcome a new King of the Jews; he is sending to have our son killed."

"But..." But it was no use. Mary could not resolve her questions. Neither, for that matter, could Joseph. But for the moment it hardly mattered. Son of God or not; Messiah or not, King of the Jews or not - the child was in danger and his life must be preserved.

They tried to rest a little but neither could get to sleep again. Within hours they were up and packing.

They awoke Ephraim and told him.

They had no chance to say goodbye to anyone else.

And they had little choice but to hope that Menci would make the long journey to Alexandria.

They crept away silently from Bethlehem as dawn was breaking. A cold and unfriendly dawn.

EPILOGUE

When Cyriacus came later in the morning he was devastated. Ephraim explained and together they stood and watched while the cohort of Roman soldiers searched the village and killed eighteen very small children.

Cyriacus returned to the hills and for the rest of his life prayed to the tiny child he had seen at birth. The other shepherds slowly forgot. Stephanos left the fields to go into business with a cousin: finding, letting and selling accommodation. He was remarkably successful.

The Magi returned to Babylon and dispersed. Melchior still watched the skies, but as an old man he felt he had done enough. They had achieved what they wanted to; paid homage to a possible new king in case it was important. Now the other Magi were on to new things and new journeys. The small child from Bethlehem receded from their minds. He would not be heard of again in their lifetimes.

Zacharias died before long. His son John would become known as John the Baptist and prepare the way for his cousin Jesus and his teachings some thirty years later.

Menci could not finish the journey to Alexandria. After fifty miles she was not only exhausted but lame too. Mary and Joseph used some of Herod's money to find a willing farmer who would keep her in pasture for the rest of her life and also supply them with a younger animal. They did not let their relative wealth show, and their apparent poverty was their saviour on the journey – they were simply too insignificant to attract any attention. In the great Egyptian seaport, they found a large Jewish quarter with its own Jewish ruler. As he had expected, Joseph discovered members of his family there and after they had used up all of Herod's money easily found enough work to look after his wife and child.

Herod survived another two years. When he died, Mary and Joseph and Jesus made the return journey to Nazareth.

They had more children – two more sons and two daughters. But a man's life expectancy was only forty-five years and Joseph died within a decade and life became very difficult for Mary. A widow was the weakest person in Judean society. With no protector and no provider, she was totally dependent upon her children. And Jesus, as the oldest, should be the most responsible.

But he wasn't there. He was already away preaching. At home, Mary's friends gossiped about the missing son who should be looking after his mother. Mary herself, unwilling to think badly of her son, began to wonder whether he was mad, surrounding himself with strange people who spoke against the rich and powerful.

He was not popular with Mary's friends and he was not popular with the authorities, who viewed him as a dangerous radical. They let him get on with it for a time and then decided enough was enough.

The boy who was born in a cave was hung on a cross thirty three years later.